All You Have Is

NOW:

How Your Approach
to the
World Determines Your

DESTINY

JOHN PATRICK HICKEY

All You Have Is

NOW:

How Your Approach
to the
World Determines Your

DESTINY

TREMENDOUS E
LIFE BOOKS.co

All You Have Is Now:
How Your Approach to the World Determines Your Destiny

Published by:
Tremendous Life Books
118 West Allen Street
Mechanicsburg, PA 17055

717-766-9499   800-233-2665
Fax: 717-766-6565

www.TremendousLifeBooks.com

ISBN: 978-1-936354-35-1

DEDICATION

This book is dedicated to my dear friends Pete and Diane Nauseda. True friendship is a great treasure. God was so good to us by putting you in our life.

ACKNOWLEDGEMENTS

I would like to thank my dear wife Kate for all the time, energy, encouragement and work she has done to help me do what I love to do. Without her, I do not know how I could have achieved so many of my dreams—since she is one of them.

Thanks also to my loving family; our daughters and their husbands, Beth & Tony, Kathy & Jeff; and our nine grandchildren, Emma, Maggie, Dylan, Ethan, Hannah, Audrey, Ayden, Noelle, and Jackson. They have made me a better man.

Special thanks to Tracey Jones and the folks at Tremendous Life Books for their expertise and kind help on this project.

TABLE OF CONTENTS

INTRODUCTION

"You must take action now that will move you toward
your goals. Develop a sense of urgency in your life."
—H. Jackson Brown, Jr.

During my years of working with people as a pastor, instructor or coach, I have seen many succeed in their dreams and many fall short. I can tell you without question that there is one key element that makes the difference between those who succeed and those who do not. That element is action. People who take action will always achieve their goals. Napoleon Hill once said, "The world has the habit of making room for the man whose actions show that he knows where he is going."

All You Have Is Now was written to help **Success-Minded People** see not only that action is important but to give some practical advice on how to achieve it. I have attempted to do this in two ways: 1) Show how to create and plan achievable goals. 2) Provide simple action steps to follow as you read the book.

All You Have Is Now is not a book to be read and put on the shelf. You must take action as you read. Have a pen and paper handy to underline and take notes. Use this book for your goal setting to help keep you focused and moving forward. It is a tool to be used, not just a book to be read. By following the steps given in each chapter you will have a clear, well written goal that you can achieve faster and with greater success than you ever thought possible. As author Dick Biggs said, "The greatest gap in life is the one between knowing and doing."

Each of us has a choice to make. Will we choose to achieve our dreams or will we choose to allow others to use us to achieve *their* dreams. Author Catherine Pulsifer said, *"You can adopt the attitude there is nothing you can do, or you can see the challenge as your call to action."* If you are reading this book, I believe you are one who sees the call to action.

All You Have Is Now will start you on your journey to a greater success in life. Action and a positive attitude are the things that move mountains and create great things. Together they will transform your life and the way you approach every goal and dream from this day forward.

Tony Robbins said, "The path to success is to take massive, determined action." *All You Have Is Now* gives you the tools to make that happen. It is my desire that you achieve all your dreams. If you become better at taking action, and better as a Success-Minded Person, then you will make us all better. The world is waiting to see what great discoveries and innovations you hold inside. The great Pablo Picasso said, "Action is the foundational key to all success."

The principles in *All You Have Is Now* and the seven areas of goal setting have helped many to set and achieve their goals. It is not a collection of ideas but of action steps, that work for myself and for others. Ralph Waldo Emerson said, "An ounce of action is worth a ton of theory." To make the principles here work you must take action—today!

Be bold. Be brave. Dream big. Have the passion for success burning in your heart and allow it to drive you to massive action. Stand straight and tall, put a smile on your face and say with confidence and determination, *"All I Have Is Now!"*

PART ONE

Nothing Happens Without Action!

*"Get action, do things; be sane; don't fritter away
your time; create, act, take a place wherever you are
and be somebody: get action."*

—Theodore Roosevelt

What is it that makes one person get so much done and others
fail to even begin? Why do you think it may take you two months
to do a job that actually only takes ten minutes to complete? What
is the one clear and proven factor that makes the difference between
those who succeed and those who do not? The answer to all these
questions is the same. It is not time or education or age or gender
or money. The difference maker is *action*.

There is a universal truth that all successful people know:
Nothing is ever done until you take action. John F. Kennedy knew
this when he said, "Things do not happen. Things are made to
happen." Sounds simple enough, but so many people just do not

seem to get it. They wish for things to happen. They hope that things will happen. They claim that things will happen. They may even demand that things happen. The fact of the matter is that until they take action to make things happen, they will see nothing happen.

Businessperson and entrepreneur Mary Kay Ash was a person of action. Married at the age of 17, she sold books door to door to get by while her husband served in World War II. After his return, they divorced. Now a single mother supporting herself and her son, she started selling Stanley Home Products. Mary Kay worked hard and increased her sales. When a promotion became available, she was passed over in favor of a man whom she had trained, so Mary Kay decided it was time to take action. In 1963, with only $5,000.00 to invest, she and her second husband started Mary Kay Cosmetics. However, before she could start the operation, her husband died. She took action in spite of her loss.

Mary Kay Ash once said "There are three kinds of people in this world: those who make things happen, those who watch things happen, and those who wonder what happened." At the time of her death in 2001, Mary Kay Cosmetics had over 800,000 representatives—all women—in 37 countries, and sales of over $2 billion. Mary Kay Ash is seen as the leading female entrepreneur in American history. She was a person who took action.

World famous inventor Thomas A. Edison was a man of action. In his lifetime, he held 1,093 U.S. Patents. He gave us things such as the phonograph, dictating machine, the incandescent light, power plants and so much more. Edison did not just invent for the sake of discovery, he was a man of method who had a plan. All of the inventions he produced were useful to the common person. He once said, "I find out what the world needs. Then, I go ahead and invent it." Few people have changed the way the world lives as Thomas Edison did. He was a person who took action.

The pages of history are filled with the names of successful men and women who changed the world and made life better for us all. New discoveries and inventions are still happening and will happen in the future. There are new and better inventions, new products and technologies. It is amazing to see all that is going on around us and it is people of action who make it all happen. From Gutenberg to Gates you can see how people with ideas who are willing to take action have changed the way we live, work and do business.

In 1843 the Commissioner of the U.S. Patent Office, Henry Ellsworth made a startling statement when he said, "The advancement of the arts, from year to year, taxes our credulity and seems to presage the arrival of that period when human improvement must end." Ellsworth overlooked two very important things:

1. He underestimated a person's ability to dream. Every day thousands of people have great and life-changing ideas. In fact, there are more ideas for new or better products and technology than could ever be counted or developed.

2. There will always be men and women of action who will make those new ideas work. Look at all that happened in the last century. We went from the first heavier-than-air flight (1903) to walking on the moon (1969). From the first experimental television (1907) to the ability to hold live meetings with people from all over the world, at the same time, on video feed over the Internet (2000).

Orville Wright said, "Isn't it astonishing that all these secrets have been preserved for so many years just so we could discover them!" He understood that the "secrets" of flight and all other things have been there all the time. The laws of aerodynamics have always existed; people of action needed to discover them and make them work. Sir Winston Churchill also understood this principle.

He said, "I like things to happen; and if they don't happen, I like to make them happen."

We live in a time when some think that education and research are the answer to all things. However, most of the greatest discoveries have been from men and women with little or no formal education. I am not opposed to formal education, in fact I encourage it, but I do not believe it is what is required to achieve something great. Success comes from action, not knowledge alone. As Kenny J. Anderson, author of the book *Common Denominators for Success,* said, "Knowledge serves no purpose if we don't take action and apply what we learn."

Ten Elements of Deliberate Action

I believe there are ten elements that go into taking deliberate action. I use the word *deliberate* because real action will not happen on its own. You must make it happen. Real, productive action must be clear, deliberate, and well planned. Otherwise it is nothing more than hit and miss with no real results. Fitness Coach Anthony Falsone said, "The key, then, is action. It's not words, it's action. It's not promises, it's results. It's not what you know, it's what you do. So accept absolute responsibility, and then act, persistently."

Chapter One

HAVE A CLEAR, WELL-DEFINED GOAL

Earl Nightingale put it simply: "People with goals succeed because they know where they're going." It all starts with the simple, yet very difficult step of setting a goal or knowing what you what. Simple, because you are defining one purpose for your life; difficult, because you have to decide what that purpose is. Napoleon Hill, author of the classic *Think and Grow Rich* said in the book he wrote with W. Clement Stone, *Success Through a Positive Mental Attitude*, "The starting point of all achievement is definiteness of purpose with a positive mental attitude. Remember this statement and ask yourself, what is my goal? What do I really want?"

For many years, I have been a pastor, life coach, and trainer; and during that time, I have heard many life questions with which people struggle. I would say that the most common question I have heard from people in all walks of life and from all socioeconomic backgrounds is: *"What am I supposed to do with my life?"* I believe that each of us was created with a purpose, a task to perform. Each of us is part of a great master plan for humankind and no one is here to be useless. God had no quota to fill, so each of us is here by design. I believe that most of us never seek out our purpose, and therefore never fulfill it.

Each person has the potential to be good and productive, yet I also know that many people never begin to tap their true potential. It is human nature to surrender to the lowest common denominator. We must purposely strive to move ahead and achieve, like a fish that fights to go upstream rather than float downstream with the rest. Being the hopeful person that I am, I believe that many will strive to be the best they can be. The world is filled with good and caring people who are positive about life and believe they can do great things. I call them **Success-Minded People**.

When asked, *"What am I to do with my life?"* my answer is always the same: *"What do you want to do?"* I believe that there is placed in us not only a purpose but also a desire to fulfill that purpose. This is the dream. Look deep within yourself, and what do you see? What is it that you have always had a desire to do? When you relax and allow your mind to wander, what is it that you keep coming back to? I believe that dream you hold is your purpose. That dream is the very thing that will complete and fulfill you.

What Do You Want?

Set aside about three hours that you can have to yourself, alone and undisturbed. Schedule it in your calendar if you must, but find the time and make sure you do not allow anything else to creep in. This focused, alone time is vital to your success in setting a clear goal. You need the time to think and to focus.

Allow your thoughts to go with the question *"What am I created to do?"* Do not think about what you will make for dinner or all that you need to do at work. Keep focused on your dream. Listen to what your heart is telling you. The dream is there and it will speak to you if you take some time to listen.

Some may find this easy. You have known your dream for years but you never really thought you could go for it. You needed someone to give you permission to achieve your heart's desire. I give you that permission. Some of you are already doing what you love and want to go deeper and be better. Hold on to that, and do not change just to change. If you are already pursuing your dream, this will help you make it clear.

There will be some who have a million things going around in their heads and can't identify their purpose because of it. Here is an exercise that can help. List all the ideas in your head—everything you want to do or think you are called to do. Make one big list. Next, go through and cross off anything that you know just sounds like fun but is not something you would do. Next, go through and cross off the things for which you have no talent or skill. Now, with what is left, ask yourself these three questions:

1. Have I wanted to do this for most of my life?

2. Am I willing to pay any price in order to achieve this?

3. Is there something that I want to do even more than this?

Be sure to cross off anything on your list that does not fit the questions. What you have left will be your answer. If there is nothing left on the list, go back and think some more.

There is something very important you must know: Your dream will always be impossible. That's right; it will be too big for you to do. In fact, if it's not impossible, it is too small. Think of all the great things we have today that were once thought to be impossible. We must see that all things are possible to those who believe. I love the words of Robert H. Schuller, who said, "It is difficult to say what is impossible, for the dream of yesterday is the hope of today and the reality of tomorrow." We will talk more about this later, but I do not want you bypassing your dream just because it's too big. You too can agree with Walt Disney who said, "It's kind of fun to do the impossible."

Once you have discovered your dream, this will be your main goal. Not your only goal, but the one to which all others will lead. Every goal you set should move you toward this goal. If they do not, even if they are good goals, put them aside and focus on your main goal. We will make this clearer later on in *the seven areas of goal setting*.

Right now, while you are still in your alone time, describe your dream in detail. Write it down. When this dream is achieved, what will it look like? Who will you be? What things will you have? How will it feel, smell, taste, and look? Get as much detail as you can. As you write this out, feel it, allow your emotions to be involved. See it so clearly that you will know it the moment you come across it. Do not worry about how it looks on paper, how long it is, or if you spell everything right. This is for you and you alone. The one thing you must be sure of is that it is recorded in detail.

Do not skip this exercise thinking you have it all in your head. The most common goal-setting mistake people make is *not writing it down*. By writing it down you make it real and you give your dream substance. Noted goal–setting expert Brian Tracy said, "People with clear, written goals accomplish far more in a shorter period of time than people without them ever could imagine."

Once you have written down your dream in detail, read it to yourself aloud. Now you can go back and edit it, make it clearer, remove things that don't work and end up with something you can read and feel every day. You have completed the first element of goal setting. Be happy, relax, and move on to part two.

YOUR ACTION STEPS

1. Write down what you really want to do.

    _____

    _____

    _____

    _____

2. Write in detail your main goal or dream.

    _____

    _____

    _____

    _____

3. Whom do you need to become and what changes do you need to make in your life to achieve this dream?

    _____

    _____

    _____

    _____

    End Result: Have a clearly defined, written goal you can hold in your hand and read.

Chapter Two

HAVE A PLAN
YOU CAN FOLLOW

There is an old Irish saying (I know because I'm an old Irish-man): *"You cannot plough a field by turning it over in your mind."* Sadly, this is what far too many people do when it comes to making plans and taking action. I believe in thinking things out and I have told many to set aside time every day to think. However, what we are talking about here is taking action. Author and success expert Tony Robbins said, "You see, in life, lots of people know what to do, but few people actually do what they know. Knowing is not enough! You must take action."

You need to pay attention to a few things if you're going to make good and determined plans. It's not a case of sitting down and writing a simple outline of what you will do. This must be a strategic, well-thought-out plan of attack. Imagine that you're going into battle. You are not going to carelessly head out to the enemy; you plan your attack and make sure it will work. You take the time to see what could go wrong and how to avoid or overcome those things. You must know what to expect, what to do, and how to do it.

So let's look at some things we need to be aware of in order to have a good strategy to move forward:

Know the Why, and the How Will Come

Before you can look at how you will make a plan, you need to understand why you are making it. Many have told me that they know what they want to do but don't know how to go about it. That's a common problem. Sometimes you need to back up and answer a different question first: Why do you want to achieve your particular dream? What is it that motivates you? You need to understand the reason why before you can know how to go about achieving it. Estate Planner Robert J. McKain said, "The reason most goals are not achieved is that we spend our time doing second things first."

Understanding the reason why you are called to a dream will help you get clarity and motivation to succeed. Tony Robbins always says, "If the why is powerful enough, the how will come." I talked about attaching emotion to your written goal back when we did the exercise on defining your main goal. That emotion will come from the why of your dream. Do you hope to add value to others? Will you make the world better? Touch others with a powerful message, or support a cause you believe in? There is always a good reason, and that reason must have power.

This reason for your dream will be the energy that moves you forward in the difficult times. Difficult times will come, I promise you that. When they do, you have to have a reason to move forward. There must be something to believe in that is so powerful you will face anything in order to succeed. Philosopher Friedrich Nietzsche said, "He who has a why to live can bear almost any how."

Your why answers the great question, *"Why am I here?"* To know the answer to that is a great feeling. It gives confidence and courage to the one who knows his or her purpose. Steve Jobs, the inventor and founder of Apple Inc., passed away in October 2011 after a long battle with cancer. Jobs was truly a great American success story and a man who believed in his purpose. "Remembering that you are going to die," Jobs said, "is the best way I know to avoid the trap of thinking you have something to lose. You are already naked. There is no reason not to follow your heart."

As you seek to discover the reason why you must succeed, there are a couple of things that do not apply. First, money is never a purpose in life. I have nothing against wealth or people making money. I believe in capitalism and that we should all make as much money as we can. However, money is not the reason we do what we do. If you believe that success is only connected to money, you will not last long. Money is the most fluid thing we have. It can be here today and gone tomorrow. Money can be the reward for efforts, but it should not be the reason for them. You must have something bigger than that.

The secret to wealth is hard work and good management. Most successful business people have earned great wealth, lost it, and earned it again. They know that money is the result of their success not the motivation behind it.

Another thing you should not use as your why is fame. If all you want to do is feed your ego, again you will be left disappointed and empty. Fame, like money, comes and goes quickly. Even if you do something great, people will forget your name tomorrow. Success-minded people understand that it is what we do for others that will last long after we are gone.

Why do you want to achieve the dream that is in your heart? Know that, and you will have the power to achieve it. It will give you the reason to work hard every day and love the work you do.

One of the most exciting things I have experienced was discovering what I was placed on this earth to do. God was very kind to me and showed me early on what I am meant to do and how I would do it. Have I achieved it yet? No, I have not. I still strive every day to add value to others and to help those I can to achieve their dreams and to be the best they can be. My prayer has long been, *"I do not want to change the world, I just want to help the one who will."*

Be Prepared!

In 1907, British war hero Sir Robert Baden-Powell gathered 20 young men together to help them learn outdoor skills and solid principles for living. This was the start of what became the Boy Scouts. In 1910, the Boy Scouts of America began and soon became one of the best organizations in the world for young men. Most of us are familiar with the Scout motto: *Be Prepared!* Do you know just what that means? Baden-Powell defined it like this: "... a Scout must prepare himself by previously thinking out and practicing how to act on any accident or emergency so that he is never taken by surprise." Three keys here: 1) Think this out. 2) Practice. 3) Never be taken by surprise.

The key to achieving any goal is to be prepared for success. I am always disappointed when I hear how many people are prepared to fail. People say they will *try* to achieve their goals. The problem with that kind of thinking is you have given yourself a way out. *"But I tried,"* you may say as if that was an excuse to fail. Those who succeed prepare to succeed; there is no other option. In the words of that great philosopher and leader, Yoda: "Do or do not. There is no try."

Legendary coach Tom Landry said, "If you are prepared, you will be confident, and you will do the job." So what does it mean to be prepared? Time to get out your pen and paper again for another exercise. Write down your main goal again. Writing it down helps refresh it in your mind and heart. Make a list of all that you need in order to make this happen. Do you need more education, training, tools, money, or to change your job? List all that you need to see the goal achieved. Now look at the list and put a check next to the things you can start doing right now. You have just prepared yourself to succeed. You now know what has to be done, and you can start doing it.

Sometimes this can be as simple as creating a space to work in that is supplied to meet your needs. Other times it can be as intense as finding a school that can train you in the area you need or finding a new job more suited to you goal. Whatever it is, you need to be ready for the process to start. Remember the words of former New York Mayor Rudy Giuliani, "Your success will be determined by your ability to prepare."

The second key in the Scout motto is *practice*. When you achieve your goal, how will you act? How will you walk, talk to others or to yourself; what will you think about? You do not want to allow your ego to run away. Most of us would say that we will not change much, but you will, and you should. Change is not a negative thing. If you think that success can change you to an ego monster, why not think that it can make you a life-changer? You could be the most generous and welcoming person around. If that were true, how would you act? Practice that. Start to think of yourself as a success. Start to relate to others as people to whom you can add value and from whom you can learn. Act the part, so that when it comes, you will know how to act and how to succeed.

The third key is *never be taken by surprise*. One of the problems people have with success that when it comes, they are taken by surprise and don't know what to do next. Many will allow success to pass by because they were not ready. Former British Prime Minister Benjamin Disraeli said, "The secret of success in life is for a man to be ready for his time when it comes." We all must be ready to do what is necessary when success comes our way.

If we believe that we can succeed and that we are ready to succeed and are convinced we will succeed, then success will find a welcome when it comes our way. Everyday should find you preparing yourself to succeed and achieve your goal. You know what to do and how to act. You have practiced how to think and talk. As Zig Ziglar says, "You were born to win, but to be a winner you must plan to win, prepare to win, and expect to win."

Mapping the Way

Now that you are ready to succeed, we need to develop your map to achievement. This is the strategy you will use to get to where you need to be. As with all strategies, this will not be written in stone; you will need to make adjustments along the way. Later we will look at being flexible and making adjustments in detail, but for now be aware that this plan will change as you go along. You are preparing your journey so you know where to go. As Louis Pasteur said, "Fortune favors the prepared mind."

You will need the list you made of the things you need to do in order to achieve your goal. Now is the time to organize that list. Making a new list, put down what you need to do first. Do you need to take a class, make a phone call, change jobs, or read a book? Don't just put the easy things first, think it over and ask yourself, *"What really has to be done before I can go to the next step?"* If it helps, work backwards. Imagine the goal achieved: what was the thing you did just before that? What was done before that step? Go all the way back to the beginning and you will have your list. This is an important part of your strategy so do not overlook it.

Thomas Edison makes this very important point: "Being busy does not always mean real work. The object of all work is production or accomplishment, and to either of these ends there must be forethought, system, planning, intelligence, and honest purpose, as well as perspiration. Seeming to do is not doing." The achievement of a goal is hard work. There is no getting around it and no short cuts. If someone tells you that you can achieve your dreams with little to no work, they are lying to you. It takes "forethought, system, planning, intelligence, and honest purpose, as well as perspiration," and nothing less.

Now that you have the list of what must be done, you can start breaking it down into doable steps. You may feel that you are not sure of all the things that need to be done, and therefore your list is not complete. That's okay. What you need is the framework to start moving. Remember that this is not written in stone. You will find things along the way that you never thought about before. The point is that you are taking action and that is the key to all success. You have a plan, a map to follow, and now you are on your way. Pastor and author T.D. Jakes said, "While a dream and a talent are important, long-term success won't happen without a plan."

As we move forward in this process, keep handy your main goal, clearly written out, along with your list of things that must be done. We will be working with this information through this whole process. Please do not fall into the trap of laziness or thinking you can skip this because you already know what to do. For one thing, if you knew what to do you would have done it. Second, if you want true success and to make a difference in the world, it will not happen by chance. It takes work—hard work. Michael E. Porter, a professor at Harvard Business School said, "If you want to make a difference...you've got to make time for strategy."

YOUR ACTION STEPS

1. Define the "why" of your goal in writing.

   _____

   _____

   _____

   _____

2. What do you need to do to prepare to succeed?

   _____

   _____

   _____

   _____

3. When you succeed, how will you think, talk, and act?

   _____

   _____

   _____

   _____

   End Result: Have a written list of things you must do to achieve your goal, most important thing first.

Chapter Three

THINK BIG— START SMALL

Now this will be the hardest part of the goal-achievement process—getting started. All the lists you made, deciding what your goals will be and writing them down, is only the groundwork. They may have taken time and some effort, but you really have not started. This line divides goal setting with goal achieving. Moreover, as J.C. Penney said, "It is always the start that requires the greatest effort."

Within goal setting, there is a common problem of people wanting to go for either big things or small things. Each on its own will lead to failure if not put in the proper perspective. When you aim only for all the big things, you tend to put the goals out of reach. It's like trying to jump over a large chasm to the other side. If the goal is too small, there is no challenge, and we lose interest and drift off into other things. The proper mix is when you learn how to think big thoughts, have big plans, and believe big things while you're taking workable steps that move you forward at a steady pace. As Vincent van Gogh said, "Great things are done by a series of small things brought together."

When I look at thinking big, I am taken to a quote by 19th century pastor and Bible teacher A.B. Simpson, who said, "Our God has boundless resources. The only limit is in us. Our asking, our thinking, our praying are too small. Our expectations are too limited." The person who will put the greatest limits on you will be you. Likewise, if you choose to remove the limits you place on yourself you will be able to do things you did not think possible.

Thinking big takes confidence and courage. It's not just grand ideas; it's big plans and a big future. People who do not believe they can achieve their dreams never will. It's that simple. You have to believe it before you can achieve it. When we look at our own resources and abilities, it's easy to fall into unbelief. Being successful isn't just believing in what you are to do, it's also believing that you can do it. Former British Prime Minister Benjamin Disraeli said, "Nurture your mind with great thoughts. To believe in the heroic makes heroes."

Thinking Big

No great work has been accomplished without some great thinking beforehand. Only those success-minded people who have the ability to believe they can achieve great and wonderful things ever have the power to try. "Nothing limits achievement like small thinking," said William Arthur Ward. "Nothing expands possibilities like unleashed thinking." You must have a goal that is impossible in order to achieve the impossible. Big thinking will give you big results just as small thinking will give you small ones. Moreover, as Donald Trump says, *"You're going to think anyway so why not think big?"*

We will talk more later about big thinking when we talk about a positive attitude. For now, I want you to understand that the key to achievement is the ability to think big and have big plans. The key to achieving those big plans is small steps. Former German Chancellor, Helmut Schmidt said, "Whoever wants to reach a distant goal must take small steps." Think of it like climbing Everest. The mountain stands before you; it is big, impossible to conquer. You know that many have lost their lives trying, but you also know that many have reached the top. The desire to reach that summit high in the clouds calls upon you. You feel the excitement racing through your blood and you believe you will reach the top. Your mind is made up, nothing will hold you back. So what do you do? You take one step. Just one, followed by another, and then another. Each step is well thought out and no bigger than a walk in the park, but each moves you closer to the top and to the achievement of your goal.

Starting Today

St. Francis of Assisi once said, "Start by doing what is necessary, then what is possible, and suddenly you are doing the impossible." The small daily steps move you forward. In my book, *Daily Thoughts: 90 Daily Readings for Success-Minded People*, I have a reading called *Living Today* that I think applies here.

> *"We talk a lot about planning and goal setting, but always remember that the action steps needed to achieve a goal can only be taken today. If you miss today, you will never get it back. All the joy and wonders the Lord has for you to discover are within the borders of today. Do not waste a moment trying to hold on to the past; it can never change or return. Do not allow the achievements of today to be missed while you wait for a tomorrow that will never come. There is only today, and today is good."*

The big thinking gives us vision, power, and direction, but it is the small steps that are the action of the process. The key thing to remember about action is that it can only happen today in the moment. What happened in the past is over, and the future is just a plan. It is in doing the small important steps that things are done.

As you move toward the achievement of your goal, the small deliberate steps must be, as climbing the mountain, well thought out and well placed. One of the best ways to do this is to write out your action plans so you can review them, make changes, and know just what you will do and when you will do it. This is what the Boy Scouts mean by *Be Prepared*. The more deliberate your action, the fewer mistakes you will make and the faster you will move forward. If you approach the process with a hit-and-miss attitude, you will miss more than you will hit. Olympic athlete Jackie Joyner-Kersee said, "It is better to look ahead and prepare than to look back and regret."

You are now a big thinker and you have the clear goal in mind. You know that you will start small and have a plan of action. All is in place for you to get moving on your goal. What's stopping you? The time for action is now.

YOUR ACTION STEPS

1. Write out what makes your goal impossible.

    _____

    _____

    _____

    _____

2. Make a list of small steps you will need to take.

    _____

    _____

    _____

    _____

3. What is the first thing you need to do?

    _____

    _____

    _____

    _____

    End Result: Have a written statement explaining why
    this goal is impossible and where your journey needs to
    start.

Chapter Four

START
RIGHT NOW!

Here is some great advice from businessman Lee Iacocca: "So what do we do? Anything. Something. So long as we just don't sit there. If we screw it up, start over. Try something else. If we wait until we've satisfied all the uncertainties, it may be too late." Action requires a sense of urgency in order for it to be consistent. You need to know that you must do something to move forward. That is why we think big. When you have a big goal that is backed with passion and enthusiasm you are willing to get things done just to bring it about.

The old saying is, *"There is no time like the present."* The reality is, *"There is no time **but** the present."* Right now is all you have to work with. Yesterday is gone. You can (and must) learn from it but you cannot relive it. You cannot go back and correct mistakes or recapture the victories. It is gone and past. Tomorrow is yet to come. You can (and must) plan for it, but you cannot live it ahead of its time. You do not fully know what it holds or how it will play out. Even the best-set plans for the future must be adjusted to unforeseen events. All you have is today for taking action. It is what you do now that matters. It is today that tells you if you learned from yesterday, and if tomorrow is possible.

I hear four main excuses for why people do not take action on their goals. I've heard them many times, and none are based in reality. When you really look into them, you see that they are covers for a lack of action. There is an old saying, *"If you really want to do something, you'll find a way; if you don't, you'll find an excuse."* Let's look at some of the excuses we give ourselves for not taking action right now:

I Am Waiting for Things to Be Right

How many times have you waited for things to be right before you start taking action on something? We wait for the timing to be right, for more money, more education, more favorable economic conditions, for the job market to get better or any one of a million things. News flash!! Things will never be better than they are right now! Napoleon Hill said, "Don't wait. The time will never be just right."

Most of the things we wait to see improve are things that are out of our control. You cannot control time, the economy, the job market, other people, the weather or anything else. God in His perfect wisdom gave you the power to control only one thing in the entire universe, and that is you. You have the power to change you, to take action, and to achieve your dreams. You have the greatest power of all—the power of choice. Even God will not interfere with your power to choose.

Never base your destiny on things you cannot control and have no power to change. There will always be something standing in your way. There will always be someone telling you that you cannot do it, it is too impractical, wait for another day, or you are just not good enough. Many times this reasoning comes from people who love us and care about us. What they are really expressing is their own fear, which you cannot change. In the end, you must do what you know you have to do. It is your dream, your purpose, and only you can make it happen or let it die. As tennis champion Arthur Ashe said, "Start where you are. Use what you have. Do what you can."

I Can't Make Up My Mind

Commitment to a goal, cause, business, or person is nothing more than the process of making a decision. What we need to understand is that decisions are made once, and then they must be maintained. Too many people make a decision when faced with a choice only to try to make a new decision the next time the choice comes around. Success-minded people make a decision to achieve a goal and never have to make that decision again. They will be faced with a choice or some new circumstances to deal with, but the decision to achieve the goal is not in question. They only have to make adjustments along the way.

Some of the best advice I have heard on the decision-making process came from Dr. John C. Maxwell, who said that the best decisions are made quickly and changed slowly. Poor decisions are made slowly and changed quickly. Some of us are good decision makers by nature. A decision needs to be made and you make it. It almost seems too easy. Yet many—myself included—are slow decision makers by nature. We feel we need to get all the information, weigh the pros and cons, and then make the decision. The reality is that the best decisions are made quickly. Follow your gut, so to speak. I guess you can say we have to make a quick decision to make quick decisions.

Making quick decisions is not the same thing as jumping ahead foolishly. We know right from wrong. If someone wants you to do something illegal or immoral, there is no decision to make. All you have to do is stay with your conviction and stand firm for what is right. If someone is in need of your help and you know you are, in fact, able to help them, there is no decision to make. You do what is right and best for others. Most people know what to do in most situations; but they tend to avoid making a decision to avoid taking action. Abraham Lincoln said, "You cannot escape the responsibility of tomorrow by evading it today." The ability to make good and fast decisions is the key to achievement.

"Nothing is easier than saying words." Arthur Gordon, author of *A Touch of Wonder* says, "Nothing is harder than living them, day after day. What you promise today must be renewed and re-decided tomorrow and each day that stretches out before you." Once you commit to how you will live, the goals you will achieve or the things you will do, you must keep that commitment every day. Success comes to the committed, not to the undecided.

I Need to Change Who I Am and What I Do Before I Can Move Forward

You have faced the reality that you cannot change anything in the universe but you. Now here is an even greater fact of life: You will never be perfect. Try as we will, it will not happen. We are all broken in some way and we all make mistakes. However, our lack of perfection is never a reason for giving up.

The fact that you are not perfect may come as a surprise to you but it is not a surprise to anyone else. This does not mean we surrender to these negative things and never seek to improve. Accepting the fact you will not be perfect does not remove the need to try to be better. The great coach Vince Lombardi said, "Perfection is not attainable, but if we chase perfection we can catch excellence." Perfection is out of our reach, but excellence is within our grasp.

Personal improvement is something for which we must always strive. You do not have to be a slave to bad habits and destructive behavior. You can change that right now if you wish. I know some are saying, *"But I tried and tried and cannot seem to change or stop what I am doing."* This may sound hard, but every battle takes courage to win. Any person who has overcome difficulties has had to make the decision to change and then stand up and do it. Dr. Norman Vincent Peale said, "Don't go crawling through your life on your hands and knees half defeated. Stand up to your obstacles and do something about them. You will find they haven't half the strength you think they have."

The life of a success-minded person is one that pursues wholesomeness, integrity and right living. It is leaving the old behind and actively living a new life, one that leads to wholeness and success. However, as with all things, you must start right where you are. You do not achieve success after you get it together. You achieve success *as* you get it together.

I Don't Have the Time Right Now

Every person on this lovely planet is unique and different. We are all made differently, have different talents and skills, have different dreams, and react to life in different ways. However, the one thing we all have in common is time. Each person who has ever lived or will live has 60 seconds in a minute, 60 minutes in an hour, 24 hours in a day and 365 days in a year. No one gets more, and no one can save even one second. It really is a perfect system. As Albert Einstein said, "The only reason for time is so that everything doesn't happen at once."

It has never been about how much time we do or do not have. It is how we use our time that counts. Even more important is that we *do* use our time. Every minute lost is gone forever. Ralph Waldo Emerson said, "Guard well your spare moments. They are like uncut diamonds. Discard them and their value will never be known. Improve them and they will become the brightest gems in a useful life." Time, like all precious things, must be used in order to benefit from its value.

The fear of not having time has caused many to rush into things and not take the time to be excellent. They see time as rushing by and they think it is more important to get things done than to do them right. Coach John Wooden rightly said, "If you don't have the time to do it right, when will you have time to do it over?" Never think that you can control or save time by not using it wisely.

I know of people who have a dream and would really love to see it achieved. Their problem is that in order to do this they need more education. They will have to go back to school for two to five years. The thought of being in school that long is too much for them to deal with. The fact is two to five years will pass in two to five years no matter what they do. It is what is at the end of those two to five years that counts. They could achieve their dream or they could be in the same spot they are in now. Seems clear to me what the answer is.

"Today is the only time you have," said Dr. John C. Maxwell. "It's too late for yesterday. And you can't depend on tomorrow." If you are to succeed in the achievement of your goal, If you are going to take the action needed to go forward, it must be today. I love the words of Dawson Trotman, founder of the Navigators, who said, "The greatest time-waster is the time getting started." Time for action!

YOUR ACTION STEPS

1. What excuses do you fall back on in order to avoid achieving your goal?

    _____

    _____

    _____

    _____

2. Write why each excuse it untrue and what you can do instead.

    _____

    _____

    _____

    _____

3. List three things you can do right away to start your journey.

    _____

    _____

    _____

    _____

    End Result: Have a written list of excuses and how they can be overcome. Have three clear steps you can start right away.

Chapter Five

DON'T
TALK ABOUT IT

Words are very powerful things. French journalist Émile De Girardin said, "The power of words is immense. Well-chosen words have stopped armies, changed defeat into victory, and saved empires." The words you speak can encourage yourself and others or cause you to fail and never reach your goals. This is what Napoleon Hill meant when he said, "Think twice before you speak, because your words and influence will plant the seed of either success or failure in the mind of another." The things you say matter. They matter to you and to those around you.

How often do we really think about what we are saying? Many times speaking is like breathing; it is something we do with little thought that we are doing it. A success-minded person who has control of his or her life is someone who thinks about what they say, when they say it, and to whom they say it. Winston Churchill said, "We are masters of the unsaid words, but slaves of those we let slip out." This statement truly applies to the achievement of your goals. The more you talk about it the less likely you are to achieve it.

Excessive talking about our plans and dreams lessens our energy to do what is needed to achieve them. By telling many people what we plan to do, we are allowing discouragement, bad advice, and fear to invade our thinking. Too much talk will rob us of taking action; without action, nothing is ever accomplished. It is as Mark Twain said: "Action speaks louder than words, but not nearly as often."

I know that this can be a bit contradictory to those who desire to achieve a main goal in life. Some who teach success principles tell you to talk to many people about what you want to do in order to be accountable to do it. We are also told that there is wisdom in many counselors. You need good advice and different points of view to make good decisions. While I understand the logic behind this kind of thinking, I believe it is misleading and makes life very complicated.

The Need for Advice

Anyone who has asked themselves *"What should I do?"* knows that there is no shortage of advice in the world. People are ready to tell you what they think and even more importantly, what you should do. Some advice is good and some not so good. It is given freely and yet is never free. Radio host Woodrow Kroll had it right when he said, "Free advice is sometimes the most costly kind."

So how can you tell what advice to take and what to ignore? When do you listen to advice and apply it and when should you nod politely and walk away as fast as you can? The answer in most cases is not what advice you get but who is giving you that advice. Just because you care for someone or you have respect for them as a leader does not mean they know the answers to your questions.

The first thing we must ask when seeking advice about our goals is what do we really want to know. Having the right questions is more important than having the right answers. We will go into the process of developing good questions in the next chapter, but for now, remember that even the wisest person can't help you if they are answering the wrong questions.

When it comes to achieving your dream or fulfilling your purpose, the question should never be *"What should my dream be?"* No one, no matter how wonderful you think they are, should tell you what your dream is. That has to come from within and only you can truly know what you are meant to do. People can help you learn how to do it, or direct you on the road that will help you achieve, but no one should tell you what that dream is.

I stress this because the world is filled with people living out someone else's dream. They may be doing what their family thinks they should do. They may be doing what someone said was the responsible thing to do. I know of many times that one person was told by another what *God* wants them to do. Each time, the person whose dream is dictated to them ends up unhappy and unfulfilled. Even if they succeed at what they are doing, they are living out someone else's dream and not their own.

A dream comes from within you. It is what you were created to do, so it has always been there. That's why I ask people, *"What do **you** want to do?"* If you search your heart, look at the thing that keeps pulling you back, you will find the very thing you were created to do. I have helped many people discover their dream, but I have never told them what that dream is. Even when I know that they are making a mistake, I encourage them to pursue their heart's desire, and in time, they always get there. Better to take the time to discover your dream than to steal the opportunity to find such a treasure.

Ann Landers once said, "Know when to tune out. If you listen to too much advice you may wind up making other people's mistakes." If you know what your dream is, stay with it no matter what. It might seem impossible, but again, if it is not impossible it's too small. Others don't have to understand it; it is not their dream. Stay faithful to it, and you will see wonderful things happen in your life.

There is a place, however, for good advice. That is part of achieving the dream. You are only as good as your best thinking and can only take yourself so far. Don't expect yourself to know how to do things you've never done before. You must learn and grow in order to succeed at any venture. Just because it is your dream doesn't mean you have all the answers. In fact, if the dream is big enough you most likely have none of the answers. You need the help of those who know, those who have succeeded in the area in which you wish to succeed.

Here you need to do a bit of research. Who has achieved the level of success you wish to achieve? This does not have to be someone in your personal circle of relationships. You may know of this person but not know them personally. You are looking for someone who is involved in the field you wish to be in and has been successful in it. Do the research and make a list of everyone you can, living or dead, and what they can help you to discover.

Now go through that list and note next to each name how you can learn from them. Can you contact them directly? Can you read the books they have written (good way to learn from those who have died)? Do they teach a seminar or class? How can you get the information you need to learn from those who know?

For those you have never met personally, you might just ask for advice. If there is a local businessperson, minister, teacher, doctor or other successful person whom you would like to meet, why not call and set up an appointment? You would be surprised at how many are willing to take some time to help someone who is working toward success. **Success-minded people** tend to be very generous with their knowledge. The reason you have not learned from them might just be that you never asked.

Here's a challenge for you. Make a list of people who are successful in your chosen field in your local area or that you think you can reach somehow. The first name on the list should be the person from whom you think you can learn the most. List about five to seven people. Start at the top and call or write and ask if they would be willing to speak with you for 20 to 30 minutes about your career. If they agree but say they only have 10 minutes, agree to that. If they say, they cannot meet with you, thank them and move on to the next name. Set up as many interviews as you can.

Here are some things you want to remember when you have your meeting. Study this list because it can make the difference between your success and failure in this process. It can also open the door to greater benefits.

- **Be on time and properly dressed.** When I say on time, I mean *on time*. Do not show up for the meeting 15 minutes early and never even a minute late. Being on time shows you are serious and responsible. You will get much more from a successful person if they know you are serious. Be properly dressed for business. It doesn't matter if you are meeting with an artist who is in jeans and a t-shirt, *you* be dressed for business. This too shows you care about what you are doing, and it shows respect for the person with whom you are meeting. Don't push this off as unimportant. I have seen too many people lose out on great opportunities just because they decided to *"be themselves"* and dress like a slob.

- **Have a list of questions prepared and rehearsed before you get there.** Sit down and make a list of questions. Think these through well. What is it that you need to know in order to succeed? If you have only one chance to get an answer that could make or break you career, what would that be? Do not ask yes or no questions, but ones that will give you a useful answer. Have as many questions as the meeting will allow. You can figure this out by practicing before you go to the interview. Practice will also help you do a better job of asking the questions and cut out pauses and the *ums* of an unprepared talk. Have paper and pen with you and write down the answers you get. Do not try to record the conversation. Make it comfortable for the person with whom you are talking.

- **Show good manners.** Be pleasant, polite, and smile. Saying please and thank you may seem like a silly thing to tell you to do, but you would be surprised how many people don't do it. Always address the person with whom you are talking to as sir or ma'am, Mr. or Miss/Mrs., and use their last name. Do not use their first name unless they request that you do so. Always remember titles like Dr., Rev., Your Honor, or Professor. Look at them when you are talking to them, and pay attention when they are talking to you.

- **Keep to the agreed time.** If your time was to be for 20 minutes, in 20 minutes, no matter what you have left unsaid, close the meeting. Thank them for their time, let them know how helpful they were, and leave. They may suggest that you talk a bit longer or that you return for another meeting. Agree to that and thank them for it.

If you can make this experience pleasant for the successful person with whom you are talking, chances are you will have another opportunity. Keep open and alert to what is going on around you and you may find this to be one of the best moves you, could have made. Say what needs to be said and no more. Remember the words of Plato, "Wise men speak because they have something to say; fools because they have to say something."

Books are also a great resource for learning. Do you realize that you have at your disposal right now, no matter who you are, more information and resources than Benjamin Franklin had in his whole life? You do. If you look at what he was able to achieve with what little he had, what is our excuse? Don't think that it's because he was smarter than you are. Studies have shown that most of those we think of as geniuses actually have average intelligence. What set them apart is a drive to learn and the ability to take action. You can hold the secrets of the universe in your hand but they are useless if you do not take action.

Not so Good Advice

One reason to be selective about whom you talk to about your dreams is not so you can keep a secret, but so you don't have to deal with bad advice. I don't think I have to tell you about those who would undermine your dreams and do all they can to see you fail. These people do not care for you and do not wish to see you succeed. You do not have to be a detective to find out who they are.

Sometimes those who love us the most can bring the hardest discouragement to our dreams. This is not because they wish us harm or are being unfair, but most likely because they fear for us. They do not want to see us fail or to be hurt and disappointed. They may listen to your dream but then say, *"That's great, but isn't it a bit unrealistic?"* There is no use trying to convince them because all they see is you falling on your face. The best way to deal with this is not to say anything at all. Let them see the dream unravel before their eyes rather than telling them what *"could"* happen. In the words of Benjamin Franklin, "Speak little, do much."

I do want to address a common piece of bad advice: the importance of having a "Plan B", a back-up plan in case you fail. Plan Bs are never a good idea because they give us a way out.

The human mind is such that if you give it a way of escape, when things get tough (and they will), it becomes too easy to quit and give up. If you cannot believe in your dream enough to stick with it no matter how difficult it gets, then you should find a new dream. I can promise you that you will fail at times, you will make mistakes, the way will be hard, and it all will take far longer than you thought it would. That is the nature of success. Victories are won; never given. Success is not easy; it's hard work. However, it's worth every bit of effort if this is what you were created to do.

In his book *Mastering the Seven Decisions,* Andy Andrews tells the story of Hernando Cortés, a Spanish explorer who traveled to the Yucatan Peninsula in 1519 in search of the gold of the Aztec Empire. The Aztecs had a fierce army who held on to their gold through many battles over 1,600 years. Cortés not only wanted to win this battle, but he fully believed he could.

Five hundred men arrived on 11 ships ready for war. Once on land Cortés did the unexpected. He ordered all the ships to be burned. He told his followers that they would either go home in the enemy's ships or die. With no Plan B, they had no choice but to win. And win they did. Andrews says, "Most people fail at whatever they attempt because of an undecided heart. Success requires the emotional balance of a committed heart. When confronted with a challenge, the committed heart will search for a solution. The undecided heart searches for an escape."

Burn your boats! There is no Plan B for you. There is no option but for you to succeed at your goal. There is no need to discuss it or to weigh the pros and cons. You will achieve your dream because it was what you were made to do.

Time to Get Started

Talking about your dream will only rob the energy that you need to achieve it. You must quit telling everyone what you are planning to do and get busy doing it. Walt Disney said, "The way to get started is to quit talking and begin doing." People will tell you all kinds of things you should not do, but only you can decide what you will do. Eleanor Roosevelt said, "Never allow a person to tell you no who doesn't have the power to say yes." Enough talk—time to take action!

ALL YOU HAVE IS NOW

YOUR ACTION STEPS

1. Make a list of those whose advice would benefit you.

   _____

   _____

   _____

   _____

2. Check off those with whom you can set up meetings.

   _____

   _____

   _____

   _____

3. Follow the instructions in this chapter to have a profitable interview.

   _____

   _____

   _____

   _____

   End Result: Know from whom you can get advice,
   what advice you need, and how you will get it.

Chapter Six

Be a
Positive Thinker

We have all heard over and over again that having a positive attitude is important to achieving success. In every book, seminar or teaching that you read, see, or hear on the subject of success you will find *positive attitude* front and center. Well, now you're going to hear it from me. Your attitude is the thing that will make or break your success, happiness, and relationships. W. Clement Stone said, "There is little difference in people, but the little difference makes a big difference. The little difference is attitude. The big difference is whether it is positive or negative."

Our attitude will determine what we will strive for, whom we will be, and how our life will turn out. Success-minded people know that you must work hard to maintain a good positive attitude. There is much in the world today that pulls us to the negative side of life. Every day we face things like negative music, movies, and TV along with a 24-hour news cycle that repeats the worst of the world's news all day long. It takes vision, courage, commitment, and a belief that you can make a difference to maintain a positive attitude. It's hard work that must be deliberate and focused, but it can be done. More importantly, it is worth the effort.

To build a positive attitude you must take some deliberate action. You must be responsible for your thoughts, words, and actions. A positive mind-set says that you are not a victim to the whims of others or by circumstances over which you have no control. A positive attitude says you are in charge of how you think and feel and that you have the guts and courage to be the free person you were created to be. Coach Pat Riley said, "If you have a positive attitude and constantly strive to give your best effort, eventually you will overcome your immediate problems and find you are ready for greater challenges."

Let's look at some of the characteristics that make up a positive-thinking person:

They Take Control of Their Thoughts

The great 19th century poet and philosopher Ralph Waldo Emerson said, "Life consists of what a man is thinking about all day." Have you ever stopped to think about what *you* think about? Here is a simple but informative exercise I want you to do. Get a small notebook or pad and as you go through your day stop every hour or so and jot down what you are thinking about. Don't analyze it or go into a lot of detail, but just a thought or two. At the end of the day, look your lists over. Are your thoughts through the day positive or negative? Do you spend more time thinking about what is going wrong or what is going right? Are you fighting battles in your mind or are you at peace? Are the things you worry about real or imagined? As Mark Twain once said, "I am an old man and I have known a great many troubles, but most of them never happened."

This list will help you to understand where your thoughts go when you do not control them. One of the interesting things about this exercise is that many see how much time they spend thinking negatively and how exhausting it can be. Those who worry and are angry in their thought-life often feel tired and worn out all the time. On the other hand, those who practice positive thinking and keep their thoughts upbeat end their day feeling refreshed, at peace, and satisfied with their productivity.

They Take Control of Their Words

Look back on the list of thoughts you made. What words did you use? Are they negative words that make you weak? Words like can't, won't, mad, disappointed, failure, impossible, should have, would have, and the like? Or are they more positive and encouraging words like can, will, excited, possible, hopeful, will do, can do? There is a great deal of power in the words we use. They can infuse us with hope and confidence or make us fearful and defeated. As Pastor Joel Osteen said, "You can change your world by changing your words...Remember, death and life are in the power of the tongue."

Look at the way you use words. First, how do you talk to other people? Are you encouraging and giving them hope that they can achieve their dreams? We have all met those who cannot help but say negative and fearful words when talking to another. *"Oh, you can't do that." "That is too dangerous." "You don't have what it takes to achieve that." "Get real! You could never achieve that."* The words ring in our head. The thing to remember is that they do not just hurt the person they are being spoken to but also the speaker. Negative, fearful people seldom achieve anything and end up with more sickness and problems that do positive people.

Speaking good words to others works in the same way. When we make it a point to always be encouraging and to build up other people you will see that people will come to you as if you are a magnet. And you are. We all long to be encouraged and to have someone believe in us. Your positive words can make the difference in someone's life. Can you remember when someone encouraged you? How long did that last? If you are like most people, it's still working today, even if the encouragement came 20 years ago. As George Herbert said, "Good words are worth much, and cost little."

Now look at the words you speak to yourself. Are you talking to yourself in positive terms or negative ones? Do you believe in your dream? Do you believe that you can achieve anything if you want it badly enough? If so, your self-talk will be positive and encouraging. Your greatest encourager must be you. You will talk to yourself in more words than anyone else will. Make it positive and believe every word.

They Take Control Through Their Actions

I am not talking about actions as in the tasks you perform or the things that you do. I want to look at how you act and move. Here is a fact: you can tell a positive person from a negative person from across a room without ever saying a word to them simply by how they hold themselves. Look around and try this. Negative people tend to be slumped over, looking down, long face, disinterested in the world. They walk slowly and avoid eye contact with others. Positive people tend to stand straight, eyes forward, with a smile or at least a bright expression. They welcome others and greet strangers as they pass. Positive people tend to walk at a faster pace and pay attention to what is around them.

Did you know that you could go from feeling bad to feeling good in seconds? Try this: Sit in a chair. Let your shoulders drop and look at the ground. Breathe shallowly and put a frown on your face. Now try to think happy thoughts. Can't do it? Well that's how unhappy people feel. Now, from the same chair, sit up straight and tall. Look forward, smile, and take deep, steady breaths. Now think sad thoughts. The result is the same. It's hard to be down with a smile on your face. If this works when you want it to, then doesn't it make sense to use your body to be happy rather than sad?

There is an old saying that motion creates emotion. I believe that this is true. If you move with confidence and power, you will have confidence and power. In workshops, I often bring a cape. I ask for people from the audience to come and put the cape on and walk around. You would be amazed by how this cape changes a person. They may be shy and reserved, but when they put the cape on they will strut, spin, and let it flow as if they had wings. Try it for yourself. If you don't have a cape use a blanket. You will see how it builds your confidence and frees you up. The secret is to walk around thinking you have a cape on all the time.

Success-minded people tend to be successful, confident, and friendly because they act successful, confident and friendly. They smile and keep eye contact with others. People feel comfortable around positive people because positive people feel comfortable with themselves. Les Brown said, "Your smile will give you a positive countenance that will make people feel comfortable around you." People like to be around happy, positive people. Don't you? When you move and act like a winner you become a winner.

They Are Grateful

Nothing builds up your attitude like gratitude. You cannot be depressed, negative, and grateful at the same time. Grateful people are positive and cheerful because they have a reason to be. Andy Andrews in his book, *Mastering the Seven Decisions That Determine Personal Success*, said, "Happiness—true happiness, that is—comes from deep within. Happiness comes from a grateful heart. It is impossible to be ungrateful and happy at the same time. Depression, anger, resentment, and other lower emotions may arise, but a grateful spirit keeps you from feeling sorry for yourself—the seeds of depression cannot take root in a grateful heart."

For several years now, I have been privileged to visit a young man in state prison. I say it is a privilege because this young man, although trapped in an environment that is less than happy, is one of the most grateful people I know. He knows it was his own bad choices that put him in prison and he does not blame anyone else (that in itself is a positive move). Yet he has learned to be grateful for what he has in the simplest things. His faith is strong so he is grateful for the work God has done in his life. He is grateful for the days the sun is out and grateful for the rain. He is grateful for every letter he gets and all visits from friends and family. His response to a treat from the vending machine during a visit is like a child at Christmas. It is always convicting to know that I who have so much, will learn gratitude from one who has so little. I am truly grateful for my grateful friend.

Albert Schweitzer once said, "In everyone's life, at some time, our inner fire goes out. It is then burst into flame by an encounter with another human being. We should all be thankful for those people who rekindle the inner spirit." Do you have someone who rekindles your inner fire of gratitude when that flame gets low? I have been blessed to know many in my lifetime. Dear friends with cancer who greet each day with gratitude. People who have suffered tragedy and loss who, without complaint, show how grateful they are for all that they have. I desire to be such a person as those who inspire me.

I believe that it is not the loss these people face that makes them grateful. It is the positive attitude they choose that makes the difference. As I said, you cannot be grateful without a positive attitude and you cannot have a grateful spirit without it giving you a positive attitude. It is a law of life. Joel Osteen said, "Choosing to be positive and having a grateful attitude is going to determine how you're going to live your life."

They Learn to Laugh

Few things will keep you positive better than a good sense of humor. Did you know that a child laughs over 300 times a day? The average adult only laughs 15 times. What's up with that? It isn't that there's nothing to laugh at. The human race is the funniest thing going. I think that God must sit in heaven and laugh Himself silly looking at us. Just go to the mall sometime, sit, and watch people. You'll love it. And of course, be sure to laugh at yourself. The old proverb is, *"Blessed is he who can laugh at himself. He will never be without entertainment."*

Success-minded people are people who like to laugh. That is why they do not live in depression or discouragement. You cannot be happy and sad at the same time. Humorist Mark Twain said, "Against the assault of laughter nothing can stand." Laughter is your weapon against the negative influences that surround you. If you learn to laugh, you will remain positive and have a good time doing it.

Laughter not only helps us keep a positive attitude but it is good for you. Dr. Norman Cousins called it *"internal jogging"*. The great comedian Milton Berle said, "Laughter is an instant vacation." Have you ever sat around with friends and just laughed about the silliest things? You laugh so hard you cry and when it's done you feel great. Laughter relives tension, releases stress and puts life's problems into perspective.

I know some think that success is serious business and you must not give in to such silliness. I think of the words of Andrew Carnegie, a man who knew what success was all about: "There is little success where there is little laughter." If you can't have fun on the road to success then why go?

One of my favorite quotes comes from Ralph Waldo Emerson. I have this written down and I read it on a regular basis because, to me, it sums up what success is really all about. Emerson said: "To laugh often and much; to win the respect of intelligent people and the affection of children; to earn the appreciation of honest critics and endure the betrayal of false friends; to appreciate beauty, to find the best in others; to leave the world a bit better, whether by a healthy child, a garden path or a redeemed social condition; to know even one life has breathed easier because you have lived. This is to have succeeded."

They Know Reality

One of the complaints about a positive attitude (if you can believe someone would see a problem with being positive), is that the positive person does not face reality. There is this image that a positive person says that all is good and they refuse to see anything bad or wrong in the world; they are out of touch with reality. On the contrary, the positive person sees life very clearly and faces the challenges straight on. The difference between a positive person and all others is that the positive person believes that they will make it through—no matter how hard it is. They are motivated to achieve their goals and to win in life. Yes, there will be struggles, but they know they can win. I love what Zig Ziglar said: "People often say that motivation doesn't last. Well, neither does bathing—that's why we recommend it daily."

Without question, positive thinking will do more for you, will make you feel better, do better, let you have more fun, and be liked by more people than negative thinking ever will. Since it is under your control, doesn't cost anything, and always has the best return, why wouldn't you do it? Being positive is a habit, a way of life, just as negative thinking is. Follow the principles outlined here and you can develop a habit of being a positive person. William James wisely said, "Sow an action and you reap a habit; sow a habit and you reap a character; sow a character and you reap a destiny."

There are three books I would like to recommend to anyone seeking to be a positive thinker. They cover six decades but are as relevant today as the day they were written. Success principles may take on different forms as time changes, but the principles themselves do not change. I suggest that you take the time to read and learn from these classic books. They hold secrets that, if applied and used, will change your life.

1. *The Power of Positive Thinking,* by Dr. Norman Vincent Peale. First published in 1952 this is foundation for most positive-thinking teachings. You will find the setting a bit outdated, but the instructions given by Dr. Peale are timeless.

2. *Success Through a Positive Mental Attitude,* by Napoleon Hill & W. Clement Stone. First published in 1960 this is one of the best and most useful of all books on positive thinking. Now over 40 years old, it is still one of the top-selling books for those seeking success.

3. *The Difference Maker,* by Dr. John C. Maxwell. This is the newest of the three books, published in 2006. Dr. Maxwell is one of today's most respected writers and teachers on leadership and successful living and this is by far one of the best works ever written on the subject of attitude, one that should be read every year by those who wish to be the best they can be. Dr. Maxwell states, "A positive attitude is an asset every day in nearly every way. It not only helps with little issues, but it also provides a positive framework from which a person can approach all of life." How you think and what you think about will affect your day more than

anything else. You have the ability to choose what you think about and what you fill your mind with.

You cannot make the world be the way you want it to be; nevertheless, you can change how you respond to that world. It is never what happens to you that affects your ability to achieve your goals; it is how you handle what happens to you. If you choose to win, if you choose to learn from life, if you choose to let the struggles you face make you stronger, if you choose to see the possibilities in life rather than the drawbacks, if you choose to smile even when life hurts, you can be a positive person. Enjoy your life; it's the only one you get. See it as President Ronald Reagan did when he said, *"Life is one grand, sweet song, so start the music."*

YOUR ACTION STEPS

1. Make a list of what you think of throughout the day.

   _____

   _____

   _____

   _____

2. List the types of words you use most often. Positive or negative.

   _____

   _____

   _____

   _____

3. Do one of the exercises for changing your emotional state.

   _____

   _____

   _____

   _____

   End Result: Make having a positive attitude a daily habit.

Chapter Seven

BE
FLEXIBLE

The Greek philosopher Heraclitus, who lived between 535 and 475 BC, said, "Nothing endures but change." Thousands of years have passed and humankind has developed and transformed into something very different from when old Heraclitus was walking around, but one thing is the same: *"Nothing endures but change."* The one thing that never changes is that everything changes.

There are two ways we can approach this reality. One is to fuss and whine and wish that everything was as it used to be. The other is to embrace change and change with it. Management expert Tom Peters said, "Winners must learn to relish change with the same enthusiasm and energy that we have resisted it in the past." Like it or not, things will change—you will change—it is only a matter of changing to the better on being left behind.

At one of my previous jobs, I was the supervisor of a department that had to face change almost daily. I developed a motto that the staff would repeat at each weekly staff meeting: *"Change is our friend!"* Change is our friend. Success-minded people learn that in order to achieve their dreams they must change and change often. These changes may be small things like how we do things or our plan of approaching a task. They may also be big changes like our attitudes and behavior in a certain area. Either way it is change and once made, we will not be the same. I love the words of former U.S. Vice President, Adlai Stevenson who said, "Change is inevitable. Change for the better is a full time job."

Are there areas of your life that need to undergo a change? I know that there are. How do I know? Because we will never grow and be able to achieve our goals unless we change—often. Jim Rohn said, "Unless you change how you are, you'll always have what you've got." Isn't that true? Haven't you struggled with an area in your life and find that you always end up in the same place? I know that I have. The wonderful secret is that it's not the behavior or attitude that has to change, it is you. That's good news because the only thing you can change is you.

I'm not talking about losing your personal identity. You are who you are and nothing will change that. The person I'm talking of changing is the part of you that is controlled by your decisions, actions and attitudes. The person who is not successful today but becomes successful down the road is still the same person. So what changes? How you think and behave. Learn to make good decisions, learn new things, and pursue the thing you were created to do. Learn to embrace change and be willing to let go of the past to move forward into greatness.

This means being flexible. There are some things that we know will change and we must be flexible to change with them.

Be Flexible to Unexpected Changes

We talked earlier about making plans and adjusting those plans when needed. I told you then and I will repeat here that your plans are not written in stone. It would be nice if life was predictable and we knew just what would happen next, but that is not how it works. No matter how good our plans are they are bound to change. I think Woody Allen was right when he said, "If you want to make God laugh, tell Him about your plans."

Just because we know that our plans will need to be adjusted does not mean we avoid making them. President Dwight D. Eisenhower said, "In preparing for battle I have always found that plans are meaningless, but planning is indispensable." Changing the plan is never changing the goal. We must always have the destination and the determination to get there set in our mind. It is the *how* we will get there that may need adjusting.

On a flight from New York to Los Angeles, the pilot is off course a majority of the time. The navigator must adjust for storms, winds and other planes, but the destination is still the same. Just because some unexpected storm comes up does not mean they decide to go to Seattle instead. The same is true with setting our goals. You have the main goal that you wrote down and read daily. You have a plan of action to achieve that goal. When the unexpected happens (and it will), you do not give up and change the goal. You adjust your plan and move forward. Napoleon Hill said, "The majority of men meet with failure because of their lack of persistence in creating new plans to take the place of those which fail."

Being flexible does not mean that you completely rethink your plan every time an obstacle gets in your way. You must recognize what is an unexpected obstacle that will require change and what is a bump in the road that you must just go through. Not being able to see perfectly into the future, you will constantly come across people and things that seem to stand in your way. Most of these can simply be ignored and bypassed. You learn to whom you should go for help and direction and whom to avoid. That does not make those you need to avoid your enemy; in fact, many of these people love you deeply. It just means that you know you will not get the encouragement and help you need, so why ask for it? The same is true for other areas of life that you cannot control. Let's say you have plans to do something outdoors. Well, you wake up and get ready to go and it's raining. Do you rethink your whole plan and start over? Of course not; you just reschedule the task and wait for the sunshine.

Dr. Norman Vincent Peale said, "Action is a great restorer and builder of confidence. Inaction is not only the result, but the cause, of fear. Perhaps the action you take will be successful; perhaps different action and adjustments will have to follow. But any action is better than no action at all." Never stop moving and never give up on your goal. Adjust and move forward knowing that a change in plans is not a change in goals.

Be Flexible to Unexpected Ideas

As we search and find our life's goal, we will most likely see only a big picture. We are drawn to an area of study or skill. As we work toward what we believe is the main goal we see things narrow a bit. We find something that catches our heart and it becomes our passion. Does this mean the goal was wrong? No, it only means that you now see it more clearly. Here's an example. Let's say Robert, a young man in his early twenties, has a goal to become a doctor. He has always been drawn to this type of career and has worked hard to get into the right school so he can pursue his goal. After several years of study, he found that research is exciting and it becomes all he wants to do. His passion for research grows and the idea of being the local MD fades away. Was Robert wrong in thinking that being a doctor was what he wanted?

Before we answer that, tell me what child thinks of growing up to be a researcher in medicine? Not many I assure you. Children do not know what a researcher does or why they do it. In Robert's journey to do what he was created to do all along, medicine lead him to the area of study that he really wanted. All he knew was that he was drawn to medicine. He thought of being an MD because that is what he believed medicine was. During the journey toward the big picture things become clearer and narrower. Someone called to education may not end up a teacher. Someone who has a passion for sports may find their fulfillment in areas of the field of play.

Many times people face a crossroad in life and struggle with the divergence of what they set out to do and what they want to do. They knew they wanted to teach history for most of their adult life. They did all the work and prepared themselves for the classroom. Now they find that there is an opportunity to work as a museum curator. It's challenging and exciting and, in their heart, it is just what they want. What do they do? Sadly, too many times they head off to the classroom only because they think that is what they are supposed to do. It's what they prepared for. They may be good at it and become a great teacher, but their dream is never fulfilled. As Henry David Thoreau said, "Most men lead lives of quiet desperation and go to the grave with the song still in them."

We must always be flexible enough to follow our heart. Remember that you only see a portion of what you are meant to do in life. The possibilities are endless and wonderful. The key is that you must take action now. Hollis Vaughn said, "A ship's rudder gives direction while the vessel is in motion, not while it sits in the port."

Be Flexible to Unexpected Discoveries

We live in a time of constant change and development. What is new today is old tomorrow. Microsoft founder Bill Gates said, "In three years every product my company makes will be obsolete. The only question is whether we make it obsolete or someone else will." To succeed in today's world you must always be thinking of what has not been thought of yet.

A common problem for those who are setting goals is that they tend to think in terms of what has been done before. The drive is to achieve what they know has already been achieved. The truly success-minded person must be flexible enough to see what has not yet been done. What can be better? What can make things easier or more useful? What can they do that no one else has done? That question leads to success.

We have all had an idea that we thought was great but no one had done it before and therefore we thought it could not be done. Then a few months down the road, we see our idea on the shelf, selling like crazy. What's the difference between us and the person who invented it? Only that they took action and we did not. Brian Tracy said, "In a time of rapid change, standing still is the most dangerous course of action."

Success-minded people learn never to sell themselves short. Never think that you do not have what it takes to come up with a life-changing plan or product. Someone will think of it and put it into reality, why not you? Every product you see, every book you read, program, seminar, movie, medical breakthrough, and on and on, started as an idea. Not just the idea of one person, it was the idea of hundreds, maybe thousands, of people. The thing is that only one of all of those people with the idea took action. There is no reason that one person cannot be you.

Here's an exercise for you. I want you to review your main goal. Now write down all of the ideas you can that have not been done before in your chosen field. Don't say there aren't any, use your imagination and create some. Write them down. Tell how they will work and what they will need to become a reality. Do as much detail as you can, no matter how wild it seems. This will start you on the road to thinking impossible things. You must think the impossible to achieve the impossible. As the White Queen said to Alice, "I've believed as many as six impossible things before breakfast." Most people don't think six impossible things in their lifetimes. If you do only four before breakfast; you are still ahead.

Albert Einstein said, "We can't solve problems by using the same kind of thinking we used when we created them." So begin to think differently. Be bold and daring in your thinking. Be willing to look like a fool in order to be the one who changes the world. Someone will change the world, someone always has. There will be a cure for cancer in the future. There will be higher forms of communication and entertainment. Someday the computer will be replaced and automobile travel will be in the history books. The question is not if these things will happen but who will make them happen. Why not you?

YOUR ACTION STEPS

1. Make a list of what obstacles you see in your path.

   _____

   _____

   _____

   _____

2. List the different careers that are in the field of study you wish to go into.

   _____

   _____

   _____

   _____

3. What can you do that has never been done before.

   _____

   _____

   _____

   _____

   End Result: Learn to be flexible to change and open to new ideas.

Chapter Eight

ASKING QUESTIONS

It is thought that the average person asks between 15 to 25 questions a day. I must be above average because I know I can ask that many before I finish breakfast. Asking questions is not a matter of weakness or of being uninformed. In fact, people who ask a lot of questions tend to achieve more and learn more than those who do not. Egyptian novelist Naguib Mahfouz said, "You can tell whether a man is clever by his answers. You can tell whether a man is wise by his questions."

Success-minded people are curious by nature. They know that there is no shame in asking questions. Many feel that asking questions makes them look foolish. Successful people, like sports legend Tom Connolly, know that this is not the case. Connolly said, "He who asks a question may be a fool for five minutes, but he who never asks a question remains a fool forever." Questions are the gateway to success and better living.

There are two types of questions I would like to focus on. One is questions you ask yourself. The other is the questions you ask others in order to gain insight and information. We know that there are other types of questions but I believe that these two areas are the questions that move us forward the quickest. It's also important to know what questions you need to ask in each area. Knowing what the right question is will give you the right answer. As author James Thurber said, "It is better to know some of the questions than all of the answers."

Questions We Ask Ourselves

Tony Robbins said, "Successful people ask better questions, and as a result, they get better answers." I might add that they also ask the best questions of themselves. In the course of the day, you ask yourself many questions. *"Should I do this or that?" "Should I go here or there?" "Should I wear red or brown?"* We are always questioning ourselves. What you need to know is, are your questions helping or hurting you?

The human brain is a wonderful thing. It will always give you an answer to the questions you ask. The problem comes from the questions you ask yourself. Your brain will only answer exactly what it is asked.

Here's an example of what I mean. When you're having trouble solving a problem, you can ask two different questions: 1) *"Why can't I get this right?"*, or 2) *"How can I do this better?"* Many think that you will get the same answer to each question since they are both basically asking the same thing. That's really not the case, and here's why.

"Why can't I get this right?" is a negative and defeating question. What it presupposes is that you *"can't"* get things right. So your mind is going to try to find an answer to that. We get answers like, *"Because you're stupid." "You don't know enough." "You aren't*

smart or talented enough." The answers will always be as defeating and negative as the questions. Henry Ford once said, "If you believe you can do a thing or you can't do a thing, you're right." "Why can't I get this right?" supposes that you cannot do it. You will not come up with an answer that helps you get it right because *that's* not the question you're asking. This works the same with all the negative questions we ask ourselves. *"Why am I so fat?" "Why does this always happen to me?" "Why can't I get a break now and then?" "Will I ever win?"*

Now look at the second question, *"How can I do this better?"* Here you will get a better answer because you have asked a better question. *"How can I do this better?"* is positive and empowering. You are supposing that you have done well so far and now you wish to improve. Your brain will go to work on positive and more productive answers. Why? Because you are asking that type of question. You are looking for improvements and new ideas, not excuses and blame. Here is the best part: your brain will come up with the answer.

I am not saying that your brain can create information you never learned. You can only give yourself the information that you already know. This is why we must keep learning and growing. However, you will be surprised by how much you already do know. Your brain is a powerful thing. Every bit of knowledge and experience you have in life is stored there. I know we sometimes think we forget things (I do all the time), however, we really don't forget, we just can't pull then to the front of our mind at time. But they are there and, given the right question, you will have what you need. It might take a bit of time but it will come. Ever try to remember a name and you just can't seem to get it, and then at 2:00 AM you wake from a deep sleep with the name? That's because your brain will not quit til it gets the answer.

This same principle works on all the questions we ask. The key is to frame your questions in a positive and productive way. Example: *"Why am I so fat?"* can be *"How can I lose some weight and become healthier?"* *"Why does this always happen to me?"* can be *"How can I do things differently so they move me forward?"* I think you get the idea.

"Why" questions tend to be more negative. We are not looking for a better way, we are asking for a reason. This is where excuses come from. Excuses are nothing more than reasons for not achieving. *"How"* questions seek direction and information. They show we are open to learn and to do something.

Questions We Ask Others

The same principle for asking positive, empowering questions rather than negative, defeating questions apply here. We often ask questions of others to gain information or to solve a problem. We believe they know something that will be useful to us; asking questions is how we access the information. Of course, there are those questions that we really do not care about an answer to; we ask them just to ask them. Best example: *"How are you?"*

Can you even count the number of times someone has asked how you are and then walked on by not even waiting for the answer? I have answered, *"The doctor told me I had three days to live, but other than that I'm great,"* And received *"That's good"* as a reply.

We need to focus on questions that *do* mean something. Success-minded people need to understand that the best way to learn is to ask questions and listen for answers. This means that you talk the least and listen the most. One way to help you do that is to assume that the person to whom you are speaking knows something that you don't. You are only as smart as your own understanding. As I said before, you cannot gain knowledge that you did not learn. Zig

Ziglar has a great way to look at it: "Everything that occurs teaches and prepares you for the next stage in life. Nothing is lost."

Learn to ask rich questions. A rich question is one that provides a well thought-out answer. You do not learn from questions that can be answered with a simple *"yes"* or *"no"*, or worse yet, a grunt. Ask questions that require the other person to think and ones that will give you the information you need.

Learning to ask a rich question is something most of us have not been taught. In school we are not taught how to question, we are taught what the answers are. British anthropologist Roger Lewin said, "Too often students are given answers to remember, rather than problems to solve." The answer means nothing if there is not a good question first.

Here are a few examples of rich questions: *"If I am to succeed like you have, what process should I follow?" "What did you have to learn to come to that conclusion?" "Tell me about your experience and what you learned from it."*

If you are meeting with someone from whom you intend to learn then you should think of the questions you want to ask before the meeting. Louis Pasteur said, "Fortune favors the prepared mind." By preparing ahead of time you can get the best information in the shortest amount of time. Have you ever talked with someone who had the knowledge you needed and walked away thinking, *"I wish I would have asked him this or that"*? Preparing questions before you meet will help reduce that problem.

Here's an exercise: Write down the name of someone you know who has succeeded in the field you wish to enter. Create three rich questions that will give you the information you need most. You only get three questions so make them good. Then go to that person, or write them, and ask your questions. Do not be afraid of looking foolish by asking the questions. Successful people know that the only way to get an answer is to ask a question. Most will welcome a curious mind. Charles Steinmetz said, "No man really becomes a fool until he stops asking questions."

Allow me to wrap this up with a great statement from author and publisher Og Mandino who said, "Take the attitude of a student, never be too big to ask questions, never know too much to learn something new."

YOUR ACTION STEPS

1. Write down the questions you ask yourself. Frame them to be positive.

   _____

   _____

   _____

   _____

2. Make it a habit to ask positive, empowering questions.

   _____

   _____

   _____

   _____

3. Create three rich questions for someone from whom you wish to learn.

   _____

   _____

   _____

   _____

   End Result: Know how to ask rich questions and get rich answers.

Chapter Nine

NEVER GIVE UP

In June of 1940, France fell to the German war machine leaving the United Kingdom to stand alone against Hitler and his invading forces. With Europe occupied and America keeping her distance from the conflict, England was facing some very dark days. However, as often happens, when things look their darkest, a hero comes to the surface. Prime Minister Winston Churchill stood tall and defiant in the face of certain disaster. On June 18, 1940, one week after the fall of France, Churchill stood in the House of Commons and delivered a speech that would rally a nation to overcome some of the greatest odds that a country has ever faced. Churchill ended his speech that day by saying, "But if we fail, then the whole world, including the United States, including all that we have known and care for, will sink into the abyss of a new dark age made more sinister, and perhaps more protracted, by the lights of perverted science. Let us therefore brace ourselves to our duties, and so bear ourselves, that if the British Empire and its Commonwealth last for a thousand years, men will still say, this was their finest hour."

"Wait a minute," someone is saying, *"I thought this was a book on taking action and now we are into World War II. You lost me somewhere."* You're not lost. Winston Churchill and the way he lead the UK during the war is the best example of perseverance there is. When faced with impossible odds, Churchill stood his ground, and would not give up. *"Never give in"* Churchill told a group of students, and the whole country, at a speech at Harrow School in October of 1941. *"Never give in. Never, never, never, never—in nothing, great or small, large or petty—never give in, except to convictions of honor and good sense."*

On your journey to achieve your dream you will face challenges that will test you to the core. I am not talking about having a bad day or something coming later than you needed it. I mean challenges like the bottom falling out of your plans, being betrayed by trusted people, or a loss from which you think you cannot recover. My friends, success is hard, hard work. You do not know what is in the road ahead, so you'd best be prepared. Zig Ziglar said, "Expect the best. Prepare for the worst. Capitalize on what comes."

See this as if you were facing a war. There are forces that do not want you to succeed. If you ignore them, they will conquer you. If you are prepared for them, you will see victory. The greatest weapon you have, and the one that will see you through anything, is a settled determination that you will achieve your dream. No maybes, no excuses, no *"I hope so",* and no *"if I can".* You must believe in your dream so much that nothing will stand in your way.

So what are the elements of our dreams that make them so inspiring that we can have such a lasting conviction? I would like to point out only four of them: something worth fighting for; belief in your destiny; belief in yourself, and belief in the rewards that await you.

Something Worth Fighting For

We have all heard the old expression that you have nothing to live for if you don't have something worth dying for. It is in each of us to live for something bigger than we are. The universe of self, no matter how popular, is far too small for a person to find happiness. Success-minded people are creative and adventurous. They need something to believe in that has value and meaning to them and to the world in which they live. Earl Nightingale said, "We are at our very best, and we are happiest, when we are fully engaged in work we enjoy on the journey toward the goal we've established for ourselves. It gives meaning to our time off and comfort to our sleep. It makes everything else in life so wonderful, so worthwhile."

This is why you must have a clearly-defined, written goal to work with. One that you believe in so much you feel it each time you think of it. Your goal needs to have meaning for you, one that it is worthwhile and worthy of your time and attention. You should have increasing passion as you work towards the goal. If your passion for the goal is at its height at the start, it will die out before you have achieved it. Goals need to build like a fire. It starts as a flame consuming all you put into it and burns hotter and hotter the more you work at it.

However, as with a fire, you must be able to control the passion. Fire can be a powerful resource for energy. It is a wonderful tool when used properly. When out of control or misused, the same fire can be extremely destructive and can destroy all in its path. That is how it is with the power of your creative mind—your beliefs. Tony Robbins said, "Beliefs have the power to create and the power to destroy. Human beings have the awesome ability to take any experience of their lives and create a meaning that disempowers them or one that can literally save their lives."

One important thing you need to do is to define why you must achieve your goal. I had mentioned that a strong enough why will give you the how, but more importantly, a strong enough why will give you the ability to face any battle. Churchill believed that if Germany were to invade England, the world as we know it would be over. He could not allow that to happen. He also believed that the English people had it in them to stand and defeat this unholy enemy. There was no room for questions in Churchill's thinking and he would not allow anything to turn him from his destiny. When Winston Churchill stood before his people to speak, he was not passing on catchphrases or slogans. Churchill meant every word he said. I encourage you to go online and listen to his speeches and feel the passion he felt when he said, "We shall go on to the end, we shall fight in France, we shall fight on the seas and oceans, we shall fight with growing confidence and growing strength in the air, we shall defend our Island, whatever the cost may be, we shall fight on the beaches, we shall fight on the landing grounds, we shall fight in the fields and in the streets, we shall fight in the hills; we shall never surrender, and even if, which I do not for a moment believe, this island or a large part of it were subjugated and starving, then our Empire beyond the seas, armed and guarded by the British Fleet, would carry on the struggle, until, in God's good time, the New World, with all its power and might, steps forth to the rescue and the liberation of the old."

It is that passion, determination, and certainty that will see you through. That only comes when you have something of so great a value to you that you would give everything to see it achieved. All of us can win the battles we face. Remember what Mark Twain said, "It's not the size of the dog in the fight, it's the size of the fight in the dog."

Believe in Your Destiny

If you were to study the life of Winston Churchill, you will see something very powerful about him. He did not just believe that

England would win the war; he believed he would lead them to do it. It was what he was created to do; it was his destiny.

When it comes to destiny people tend to get all spooky and act as if it was something out of their control. We have images of Darth Vader speaking to a resistant Luke Skywalker, *"It is your destiny,"* as if poor Luke (or poor you for that matter), can do nothing about it. Destiny is something that is fixed and chosen for you. There is really nothing you can do but surrender to it. The reality is that nothing is farther from the truth.

American statesman William Jennings Bryan said, "Destiny is no matter of chance. It is a matter of choice. It is not a thing to be waited for; it is a thing to be achieved." The idea that your destiny is out of your control is part myth (that you live as a victim of things out of your control) and part excuse (so you do not have to take responsibility for your actions). If you were to wait for your destiny to kick in, nothing in your life would happen at all. Sadly, there are thousands of people who do just that and get those results—nothing.

I believe that each of our lives has a purpose. You have something to do that is unique to you. However, that does not mean that you will have to do something you hate or that you have no choice in the matter. Your purpose is the thing that will make you complete as a person. Therefore, it is not something negative; it is, in fact, the very thing you desire to do. Unbelievably, there are people who think that if they really want to follow a certain career choice that it must not be the right one. That's silly. The only true way to know if something is your destiny in life is if you cannot do anything else—or you do not want to do anything else.

Each of us is born with free will and no one can take it away. Even God will not take it from you. The choice is yours and yours alone. If you end up doing things that others have told you to do it is because you choose to do it. The greatest power in the world is choice. It is also the thing you will be the most responsible for. People often run from that responsibility.

Success-minded people know that they make their own destinies. As Jack Welch, former CEO of GE said, "Control your own destiny or someone else will." If you are in control then you can choose never to give up. Margaret Thatcher said, "You may have to fight a battle more than once to win." That is easier to do when you know that it is a battle you choose to fight.

Believe in Yourself

This is not an ego thing. Believing in one's self is knowing that you have the talent and ability to do what is necessary to achieve your goal. It is knowing that what things you lack you can learn or find access to along the way. It is knowing that you can do this. Ego thinks you are better than anyone else; belief thinks that you are the best you that you can be.

Ego is proud and wants to see others fail as much as it wants to see you succeed. Believing in yourself is humbling and desires to see everyone succeed as well as yourself. "Humility," Pastor Rick Warren said, "is not thinking less of yourself, it is thinking about yourself less." Believing in yourself enables you to think of others and realize that their success is not a threat to you. In fact, the better others do the better you will do.

Belief in yourself comes from a positive attitude that sees life as worth living and that you have a wonderful part to play in it. William James said, "Believe that life is worth living and your belief will help create the fact."

When things get difficult and the challenges of life come, the ones who believe in themselves will be able to stand. The ones who are convinced that they can weather the storm and that they have what it takes to succeed will see victory in the end. Determination does not allow for doubt or self-loathing. Determination knows that you can do what it takes, even if that is hard or frightening, in order to achieve the goal you seek. Inventor Charles F. Kettering gave great advice when he said, "Believe and act as if it were impossible to fail." Only those who believe in their ability to win can do this.

Believe in the Rewards that Await You

While money, fame, power, and recognition are not the driving forces for achieving your goal, they are some of the rewards that come with achievement. I love how Zig Ziglar put it: "Money isn't the most important thing in life, but it's reasonably close to oxygen on the 'gotta have it' scale." The rewards are not the reason we strive for our goals, but they sure do help and will keep us in the fight when things get tough. Napoleon Hill said, "Effort only fully releases its rewards after a person refuses to quit."

Rewards are the result of our work and achievements. They are never an obstacle to us; the obstacle is how we respond to them. If the reward of money makes us greedy the answer is not to remove the reward, it is to examine why we are greedy. If a person is self-centered and greedy when they're poor, they most likely will remain so when they're wealthy. If a person is generous and giving before they gain wealth, they will be after as well.

Booker T. Washington said, "No man, who continues to add something to the material, intellectual and moral well-being of the place in which he lives, is left long without proper reward." As our goals are achieved, so are our rewards. They go hand in hand and should not be looked down upon. Nothing is wrong with wealth and power if earned and used well. Henry Ford said, "Wealth, like happiness, is never attained when sought after directly. It comes as a by-product of providing a useful service."

Allow the rewards of your achievements to move you forward. Celebrate them and cherish them. They are blessings for you to enjoy. There is one caution I would pass on to you. Don't let the rewards, no matter how great they may be, stop you from moving forward. That's the subject of the last chapter in this section and one that is vital to your continued success.

YOUR ACTION STEPS

1. Write down clearly why you must achieve your goal.

    _____

    _____

    _____

    _____

2. Make a list of challenges you may face in your journey
    to your goal.

    _____

    _____

    _____

    _____

3. Write down the rewards you will gain by achieving
    your goal.

    _____

    _____

    _____

    _____

    End Result: You are determined never to quit. Never
    give up until the goal is achieved.

Chapter Ten

THE ENEMY
OF
SUCCESS: SUCCESS

Success-minded people know that the greatest enemy to today's success is yesterday's success. What do I mean by that? Well, many are willing to strive and work to succeed, but once their success comes, they stop trying. You cannot live off of past success. Once you stop striving, you start to go backwards. You can never stand still. As IBM's Thomas J. Watson said, "Whenever an individual or a business decides that success has been attained, progress stops."

This is why a fresh vision is so important to those who desire to keep success growing in their lives. Successful people look beyond the current goal to see a life of repeated successes. Author J. Oswald Sanders stated, "Eyes that look are common; eyes that see are rare." Too many people just want to get the goal achieved, the job done. They think that once they have finished, the work is over and they can relax. Success-minded people see that the job is never done. Today's success is the stepping-stone for tomorrow's success. As long as there is breath in their lungs, they have a new goal, a new dream to achieve. Successful people heed the warning of Doug Ivester who said, "Never let your memories be greater than your dreams."

It's when we have a dream that is bigger than what we can achieve that we have the greatest success. Fresh goals and dreams give us life and move us on to greater things. Speaker and entrepreneur Jim Rohn tells us, "If you go to work on your goals, your goals will go to work on you. If you go to work on your plan, your plan will go to work on you. Whatever good things we build, end up building us."

Do not allow your thoughts of what *was* to steal what *can be*. You cannot recapture the past, even the good parts. What was yesterday's victory is only today's memory, nothing more. Any military professional, businessperson or athlete will tell you that if you see today's victory as the end, tomorrow you will lose it all. You must feed on the energy and the excitement of today's adventure in order to move with power into tomorrow's challenge. Athlete Bill Copeland said, "You've removed most of the roadblocks to success when you know the difference between motion and direction."

There is a simple success formula that success-minded people must follow: Learn from the past, and leave it behind. Plan for the future, and keep the vision clear. Live today, and make it happen. The past is a memory, the future is a dream, but today there is action. Microsoft founder Bill Gates said, *"Success is a lousy teacher. It seduces smart people into thinking they can't lose."*

The computer industry is an excellent example of how resting on your past successes can rob you of all you have achieved. Computers and all related products that are new today will be obsolete in months. Gates knows that if he rests in his current success, he will be out of business tomorrow. Gates said, "In this business, by the time you realize you're in trouble, it's too late to save yourself.

Unless you're running scared all the time, you're gone." Many times, you will work harder to maintain success than you did to get there in the first place.

One of the best ways to combat the mistakes that rob you of your success is to understand the myths many people have about being successful. I want us to look at only three of them. They are: 1) You can stop working; 2) You can rest in your success; 3) You can stop setting goals.

You Can Stop Working

I have always found it odd that some people will work long and hard, neglecting their family and health for one goal—not to work. Where is the sense in that thinking? What good is retirement at 40, or 50, or even 65 if you are sick and alone and in reality achieved nothing but the money you thought you needed so that you could do nothing. Henry Ford said, "Any business (or person) that makes nothing but money is a poor business."

If I have not stepped on your toes so far in this book, I most likely will now. I want to talk about the whole idea of retirement. The idea of retirement really is not that old. It originated in the late 19th and early 20th centuries; however, it was not a common practice for all workers until the mid-twentieth century. Nowadays it is expected that a person will retire at 65.

I do not believe we were created to retire. We were created to achieve, create, and produce all of our life. Now I am not saying that a person is wrong to leave their job in order to enjoy the fruit of their labor and to do other things. Really, this is a personal choice and I am not making a judgment one way or another. What I am saying is that for many, retirement is not necessary and that to be able to continue to work means a longer and more fulfilled life. We all know the stories of people who were active and in good health who retire and die shortly after. Many times, it's simply that they lost their purpose. We are not created to be without purpose.

Irish playwright George Bernard Shaw said, "We don't stop playing because we grow old; we grow old because we stop playing." Successful people learn that they can be just as productive (if not more so) in their 70s or 80s as they were when they were younger. C.S. Lewis said, "You are never too old to set a new goal or dream a new dream." That is very true and the understanding of that principle means the difference between life and death for many.

Many believe that they can start doing what they love to do once they retire. My question is, why wait? Why should you save the best of your life for the end of your life? The great D.L. Moody once said, "Preparation for old age should begin not later than one's teens. A life which is empty of purpose until 65 will not suddenly become filled on retirement." This is why we need to teach goal setting and the importance of finding your purpose to our young people. Fulfillment is meant for our whole life not just our later years.

Success expert Peter Lowe said, "The most common trait I have found in all successful people is that they have conquered the temptation to give up." Look at the lives of the most successful people and you will find that they did not stop achieving even though many had more money and possessions than they ever dreamed of having. Their drive is not so that they can *have* more, but so that they can *be* more. Successful people have a need to keep achieving, becoming better, and doing what others think is impossible. Professional tennis champion Arthur Ashe said, "Success is a journey, not a destination. The doing is often more important than the outcome."

You Can Rest in Your Success

Let's just say that you have succeeded and now you have the money and time you always dreamed of. So what would be so bad to just enjoy that and stop working? After all, isn't that why people work so hard to succeed? Well, it really is not the reason most success-minded people work so hard. The rewards of success are nice and they should be enjoyed but they will never give the sense of purpose that simply achieving the goal will.

This is the deceit of the success myths: You have earned the rewards and now you should do nothing more. If you can learn anything from success it's that you have achieved something worthwhile and there is more yet to come. You have known what it is to work hard and how to overcome difficulties to achieve a dream. Do not allow the success of that dream rob you of an even greater goal. Bill Gates said, "It's fine to celebrate success but it is more important to heed the lessons of failure."

One of the sad realities of this myth is that people are more likely to give up after achieving small goals rather than great achievements. They think that they can rest before going on to the next goal. They worked hard and need to rest. The reality is they never start again. Success comes from a constant flow of achievement, not something that is on and off when things get hard. Lance Armstrong said, "Pain is temporary. Quitting lasts forever."

Successful people do not quit just because they have seen a victory or two. They know that there is a greater success ahead and they are pulled to achieve again and again. As author Maxwell Maltz said, "We are built to conquer environment, solve problems, achieve goals, and we find no real satisfaction or happiness in life without obstacles to conquer and goals to achieve."

You Can Stop Setting Goals

Success-minded people are habitual goal setters. It is something they do on a regular basis. For those who have made goal setting their habit, they find themselves more motivated, more strategic in their actions, and better achievers. They are people of vision who strive for greater and greater things in life.

John Dewey said, "Without some goals and some efforts to reach them, no man can live." Goal setting is more than deciding what you want to do in life; it is deciding how you want to live. Goal setting gives us direction and purpose. It provides the reasons for getting up each day and aggressively pursuing things that are greater than our selves. John C. Maxwell said, "Successful people conquer their feelings and form the habit of doing things unsuccessful people do not like to do."

The practice of goal setting gives us the vision to expect more in life than just the occasional victory. Once we stop setting new goals we find we have no place to go and action stops. George Whitefield said, "Press forward. Do not stop, do not linger in your journey, but strive for the mark set before you." That mark will not just appear to you from nothing. You have to put it there. You must set the goal or there will be nothing but an empty space for you to move toward.

YOUR ACTION STEPS

1. Write down what you have learned from past successes and failures.

   _____

   _____

   _____

   _____

2. On a calendar, mark the dates (3 times a year) what you will review and update your goals.

   _____

   _____

   _____

   _____

3. What is the next big goal you have planned?

   _____

   _____

   _____

   _____

End Result: Allow your success to be the catalyst that will move you to greater success in the future.

If you have read this far in the book, you know that you are a person of action. Reading, learning, and growing are all action steps that move you rapidly toward your dream. You are a person who will succeed because you are willing to do what it takes to succeed. The more you do the more you get to do. Jonas Salk said, "I feel the greatest reward for doing is the opportunity to do more." That is the feeling of a success-minded person.

In part two we will look at the seven areas of goal setting. This will help you to bring all the areas of your life under control and move you toward your main goal in life. With each step you take, you will learn more and more about your purpose and the gifts you have to give. Successful people don't have all the answers, but they know that in time they will discover them. It is as Earl Nightingale said, "All you have to do is know where you're going. The answers will come to you on their own accord."

I am so excited for you. I believe that you will do great things and things you never knew that you could. How do I know that? Because you were created to do great things. You are here to achieve that dream and I expect nothing less than full success for you.

Allow me to close this section with the words of Og Mandino. Make this your battle cry that starts every day.

"I am here for a purpose and that purpose is to grow into a mountain, not to shrink to a grain of sand. Henceforth I will apply all my efforts to become the highest mountain of all and I will strain my potential until it cries for mercy."

PART TWO

The Seven Areas
of
Goal Setting

"No matter how carefully you plan your goals they will never be more than pipe dreams unless you pursue them with gusto."

—W. Clement Stone

John C. Maxwell said, *"The secret to your success is determined by your daily agenda."* While your main goal is a long-term plan, it's your daily goals that will move you forward. There are seven areas of daily life for which you should create goals and plans.

The Seven Areas of Goal Setting

1. Personal development
2. Spiritual development

3. Vocational development

4. Finances

5. Family

6. Health

7. Fun

These seven areas are the stuff life is made of and without them you would never achieve your main goal or dream.

Chapter One

LEARNING
TO CHUNK

As we look at the seven areas of goal setting, I know what you may be thinking: *"How in the world am I going to have time to work on seven different goals at the same time?"* That is an excellent question. The fact is that it's easier than you think. You're really only working on your one, main goal which, in turn, affects other areas of your life. It seems complicated at first, but as we explain it, you'll see how it falls together. I like to call it by a term I learned from Tony Robbins: *chunking*.

Chunking is the ability to put several different steps into one act. A great example is driving a car. You may remember how complex everything seemed when you first learned to drive. You get in, fasten the seat belt, adjust the rear-view mirror, then the side mirrors, insert the key, start the car, put it into gear, look to the right and left before you go, let up the break and hit the gas. While driving you are keeping your eyes on the road, checking the mirrors, watching your speed, and following the directions to your destination. By my count, that's about 16 steps, and I'm sure I left something out. That's a lot to do, right? Today, now that you have been driving for a while what do you do? You drive the car. You don't think of all the steps, although you still do them. You do them as a single act—you *chunk them*.

This is true with most of our daily activities. It's how we get dressed, work, and make dinner. They all have many steps that we blend into one act. The same is true with goal setting. We will look at many steps but they all blend into one act that moves us forward every day. What was once overwhelming becomes easy and fast. It's all a case of learning something new and going beyond what we know to something we did not know. As author Tom Krause said, *"If you only do what you know you can do—you never do very much."*

Take a few moments and check this out for yourself. It will help you better understand how chunking works. Get your note pad and pick a daily activity: getting dressed, doing your make up, driving to work, cooking dinner, anything. List all the steps it takes to do this task. Now look at the list and see how many of these steps you think about when you do the task. Most likely, you don't really think of any of them. You are aware that you do them, but you do it as one action, not 16 different actions. Can you see how this applies to any area of life? New learning may seem hard but soon becomes as natural as walking down the street.

Chapter Two

THE RIGHT
QUESTIONS

In Part One, we talked about the importance of asking the right questions. Our brain will give us an answer to any question we ask. If we ask disempowering and defeating questions we will get disempowering and defeating answers. As we set goals for the main areas of life, we want to ask questions that empower and strengthen us. We want to ask questions that move us forward and give us clear vision. *"The important thing,"* said Albert Einstein, *"is not to stop asking questions."*

As we look at the seven areas of goal setting, remember to ask the following questions for each area. The answers will help you to create a strategic plan that will move you toward your main goal. It is key that you have your main goal before you, written out clearly, as you work on each daily goal. In each area of life, our daily goals should be moving us toward our main goal. Each of the daily goals work together to help us achieve our dreams. You don't really have seven or more goals all at once; you just have several daily steps that help you to achieve the one main goal.

These questions are meant to help you think and to become more creative in your discoveries. As you answer the questions, you will become more confident and skilled. Oliver Wendell Holmes said, *"A mind that is stretched by a new experience can never go back to its old dimensions."* Make those new discoveries about yourself and you will never think the way you did before.

The answers to these questions will help make a clearer picture of where you are going and what changes you need to make. The answers will also show you if you are off course. If the answers conflict then you really need to step back and reevaluate your goals and why you feel you need to achieve them. See these four questions as a measuring stick that will help you see progress and keep you going in the right direction.

Question 1: Who Must I Be?

Ask yourself, *"What kind of person do I have to be to achieve this goal?"* Should you be more aggressive, more positive, and more confident? Think of others who have already achieved and think about their character qualities. What is it about them that stand out? Remember, you are not looking for what you must get rid of in your life, but what you must become.

"Yes, but I am who I am, and I cannot change." That's only partly true. As Popeye said, *"I am what I am and that's all that I am."* You are not trying to change your personality; you're trying to change your behavior. All success-minded people change their behavior in order to achieve their dream. We were created to change and improve. A.W. Tozer said, *"You do not have to continue to be as you are—you can be different! You're not fixed like concrete but pliable like clay."*

If you had already achieved this goal, how would you behave? How would you act around other people? How would you hold yourself, walk down the street, or face difficulties? I want to stress that you are not concerned with what you should not do but with what you *will* do. Success is never built on not doing things, only on doing the right things. Keep the question positive; you are improving, not recreating. John Wooden said, *"Do not let what you cannot do interfere with what you can do."* The old behavior that may have held you back will drop away once you replace it with empowering, positive behavior. The two cannot exist together. It's what you choose to do that counts, so choose well.

Question Two: What Must I Learn?

Oftentimes our goals require us to learn new skills. Learning is the action that makes the greatest difference. Success-minded people are consistent students, always learning and always growing. Peter Drucker said, *"We now accept the fact that learning is a lifelong process of keeping abreast of change. And the most pressing task is to teach people how to learn."*

In order to achieve your goal do you need more education, more skills, to learn a new trade, get a new job, or learn a new language? What do you need to know that you do not know now in order to achieve your goal? Do not allow the things you do not know to become an excuse for not going after your goal. If there's something you need to know, learn it. Chemist Willis R. Whitney said, *"Some men have thousands of reasons why they cannot do what they want to, when all they need is one reason why they can."*

Not knowing something, or the need for more training and schooling, has been one of the most destructive excuses people have had for failing. If you need more training—get it. Do what it takes to learn all you can so you can succeed. If your goal means going back to school for five years then do it. Five years will pass no matter what you do. It is what you do in that five years that matters.

Each step you take to learn more is another step toward success. It's what you do today that matters most, not what you do five years down the road. It is in taking action that you will gain the power to succeed. Andy Andrews said, *"There are generations yet unborn, whose very lives will be shifted and shaped by the moves you make today."*

Question Three: What Action Must I Take?

In just a few short pages, you will be done with this book. What will you do at that point? Will you mark it down as another book read or will you take action to put these principles to use? Henry David Thoreau said, *"A truly good book teaches me better than to read it. I must soon lay it down, and commence living on its hint. What I begin by reading, I must finish by acting."* It is never what you learn but what you do with what you learn that counts.

Here is a principle that I have personally found to be helpful for goal achievement. Whenever you set a goal, do something toward its achievement within 24 hours. Gather information, make a phone call, set an appointment, do anything as long as it moves you toward the goal. This can be something big or small, but it must be sincere action toward the goal. Do it within the first 24 hours.

When we put off taking action, it weakens the goal and most of the time it is never achieved. Delay action and you may not get to it for months; however, act in 24 hours and you will keep taking action until the goal is achieved. Businessman and hotel chain tycoon Conrad Hilton said, *"Success...seems to be connected with action. Successful men keep moving. They make mistakes, but they don't quit."*

Nothing that you have learned from this book or from any other book or person will mean anything if you don't transform the information into action. The poet/philosopher Goethe said, "*Knowing is not enough; we must apply. Willing is not enough; we must do.*" You can have all the very best intentions to achieve your goal but if you do not act, act often, and act continually, it will mean nothing. Action is the key to all success, no exceptions.

Question Four: What is My Timetable?

Napoleon Hill said, "*A goal is a dream with a deadline.*" That is so true. One of the things that transforms a desire into a goal is that all goals have deadlines. Goals were created to be achieved. There is always a time when the work is done and that particular goal is accomplished. The wonderful thing about goal setting is that you can choose when you want the goal to be achieved.

Timelines help us to see if we are progressing toward our goal. You should be able to look at your goal and see that you have been moving forward. A timeline also motivates us to get to work. Time-lines should never be unreasonable or stressful. You cannot change the world in a weekend. At the same time, they should make us stretch and push us to work in order to keep them. A timeline should only be changed when there is excellent reason; the thing to remember is that they *can* be changed.

Success-minded people know that setting a timeline for a goal is like hearing the starting pistol for a race. You know the destination and when you have to be there, so you start to run. Yes, some people get a bit ahead of themselves and have to backtrack a bit, but that's okay. I believe in the old saying, "*It's better to be one who is told to wait than to be one who waits to be told.*"

Some timelines will be set for you. For example, if your goal requires you to go back to school and get a degree, you will need to work within the guidelines of the school. If your degree will take four years, then your timeline for that part of your goal is four years. In some ways, this is helpful because you can plan your goal-achievement accordingly.

At other times, the timeline will be very hard to set. There are many things you cannot control like the weather, traffic, and other people, any of which can delay or speed up what you are trying to achieve. Set a timeline with this in mind and do your best to stick to it, but be flexible. Stressing out over things you cannot control is useless and will work against you. Remember that the one thing you can control is how you handle the things you cannot control.

The key to making timelines work is to take action every day. Just having a date will do nothing; you must take action to achieve something by that date. Even if you only do something small one day and something major the next, keep taking action. Former Chaplain to the U.S. Senate Peter Marshall said, *"Small deeds done are better than great deeds planned."*

Chapter Three

THE SEVEN AREAS
OF
GOAL SETTING

Each of these seven areas represents a different part of our lives. Together, the goals that you set will all move you toward your main goal. We humans are very complicated beings. To keep in balance and find true success and happiness we must take into account each area of our lives. If we achieve in one area and leave others empty, we will not achieve the success we seek.

A word of instruction here: As you start to look at the seven areas keep your notebook and pen handy. Give each area its own page in your notebook so you can brainstorm and collect ideas. Remember the four questions from the previous chapter and answer for each of the seven areas. Make a list of all of the things you wish to achieve in each area. Once you have made the lists, put them in order by importance. Keep the list to no more than 10 goals for each area.

Take the top three goals from each area and write them on a separate sheet under the title of the area. It will look something like this:

Personal Development Goals

Read 20 books in my area of interest this year.

Take a class in _____.

Attend two seminars on _____.

Do not do more than three goals per area. Setting too many goals will be self-defeating. Keep the rest of the 10 goals you set on their original lists. Once you have achieved a goal, replace it with another (more on this later).

1. Personal Development Goals

These goals are designed to help you to develop as a success-minded person. Just as a successful business must have a good business plan, you, too, need a good success plan. How will you grow and learn? What books will you read? What is your plan for nourishing your inner self? Philosopher Johann Wolfgang von Goethe said, *"One ought, every day at least, to hear a little song, read a good poem, see a fine picture, and, if it were possible, to speak a few reasonable words."*

Your personal development is far too important to leave to chance. You need to know what you want and what you need to do to achieve it. Some ideas you may want to look at are:

- Learn a language
- Follow a course of study
- Get a degree

- Improve your vocabulary

- Learn a new skill

- Improve your manners or change your behavior

John Dryden said, *"We first make our habits, and then our habits make us."*

2. Spiritual Development

Every teaching you will ever read on success will tell you the importance of spiritual as well as personal development. This doesn't mean that you become more religious, but that you cultivate an ability to connect with your creator and with who you were created to be. Martin Luther said, *"This life, therefore, is not righteousness but growth in righteousness, not health but healing, not being but becoming, not rest but exercise. We are not yet what we shall be, but we are growing toward it. The process is not yet finished, but it is going on. This is not the end, but it is the road. All does not yet glean in glory, but all is being purified."*

Some of the goals you may like to set here are:

- Study Scripture

- Take a course

- Pray and meditate

- Become more involved in a house of worship

- Seek better understanding of your beliefs

The one difficult area in spiritual development is the timeline. Some things, like serving God or developing a greater understanding of Scripture, really are never done and you cannot put a deadline on them. However, it is still good to add them to a goal list that will cause you to improve and grow on a regular basis.

3. Vocational Development

What is your dream job? Is it the one you have now? If so, how can you become better at what you do? Do you want to find another job or start your own business? Then what do you have to do to make that happen and how can you become excellent at your current job? These are some of the questions to ask when looking at your vocational goals. Vocational development is the process of growing and improving your work skills, habits, and ethics. It is becoming great at what you do.

Let's face it, we all have to work. Success-minded people know that they must work for a living and that sitting around is not an option. Since you have to work, why not do something you love? No one should be in a job they hate. If you cannot find a job you love, create one. As with all things, the only way to change your vocation and make it better is to take action. Even if you are already in the career you love, you must set goals to become better at it. Excellence is always the standard of the success-minded person. As Will Rogers once said, *"Even if you are on the right track, you will get run over if you just sit there."*

Vocation development goals could include:

- Do what you have to do to get the promotion you want
- Take a class
- Get more training
- Get on a special team
- Step out and take a risk
- Create your own business

You can set many goals in this area. The key is to stay positive and ask empowering questions, not "How can I get out of here?" questions.

In *Success Through a Positive Mental Attitude*, Napoleon Hill and W. Clement Stone said, *"A person with a positive mental attitude aims for high goals and constantly strives to achieve them."* Aim high, work hard, and you will find great satisfaction in all you do.

4. Financial Goals

When it comes to financial goals, many people make two very common mistakes. They aim too high and they are not specific. I knew a young man who was starting his own business. As we worked together on setting his goals he decided he wanted to make 10 million dollars in the first year. Now I believe in dreaming big (remember what I said about impossible goals) but when it comes to finances I believe in setting goals that are achievable. Unless you are starting with 5 million in the bank, I believe 10 million dollars is just not realistic.

I have also seen several people who talk of financial goals in very vague terms. They *"want to be comfortable"*. What is comfortable? For one it can be 50 million dollars and for another it is 500 dollars. Goals need to be as specific as possible. This is where planning comes in. Determine what is possible for you to earn in a year. Now double that and put down a number you can reach. If you hit that number in a month, then double it again and keep moving. It is always better to add on to a goal than it is to pull back. When we add a new goal because the old goal has been achieved we are encouraged and positive. When we have to pull a goal back because it was not realistic we become discouraged and loose needed energy.

Success-minded people understand that the creation of wealth is not just about putting a number on paper and hoping you'll find a check in the mailbox. You need to have a plan to achieve wealth. It means becoming better at what you do so you can draw wealth to you. Jim Rohn said, *"Income seldom exceeds personal development."* You have to be worth the money you wish to attract. Therefore,

ALL YOU HAVE IS NOW

your personal, spiritual and vocational goals must be in harmony with your financial goals. Together they will move you forward. Can you see how they all work together and how important it is to think this process through?

Your financial goals can be things like:

- A target amount that you'd like to earn
- A target amount that you'd like to invest
- A target amount that you'd like to give away
- Get out of debt
- Earn a car or a vacation

Anything that involves finances will go in this area. Just keep it reasonable, challenging, and well thought out. As Andrew Carnegie said, *"Wealth is created from deeper knowledge and better thinking."*

5. Family Goals

George Bernard Shaw said, *"A happy family is but an earlier heaven."* There are no relationships that are more important to your success than those in your own family. If they are good and your family is happy, all of life is good and happy. If family relationships are stressed and broken, all of life is stressed and broken. Just as a happy family can be heaven on earth, an unhappy family can be hell.

Here is the good news: you can control the happiness in your family. I know I have said many times that you cannot control other people and I am not implying that you can fix broken family members. What I *am* saying is that you can control yourself and how you respond to your family. If you are positive and encouraging to your family, they will respond in kind.

Family goals are things like:

- Build a better life for my family
- Do more activities together
- Encourage and help my family to be their best

Most family goals are not self-focused but are directed to the betterment of others; not forcing our vision on our family but rather finding ways we can make our family stronger and happier.

Your family goals will work with the other goals to help us achieve success. Zig Ziglar said, *"People who have good relationships at home are more effective in the marketplace."*

There are many who are single and will say they have no family. We all have family. You may not live with your family but you can still work at healthy relationships with them. This area of goal setting can also be used to improve relationships with friends and others to whom we are close.

6. Health Goals

Tony Robbins said, *"You don't want to run out of gas half way up the hill of success."* Success takes a lot of work and one really needs to be healthy and strong to do their best. Robbins went on to say, *"The higher your energy level, the more efficient your body. The more efficient your body, the better you feel and the more you will use your talents to produce outstanding results."* Good health, a high energy level, and a positive attitude will take you all the way to the top.

Far too many success-minded people forget the area of health when setting goals. They see the work success calls for and the time and energy it requires but they never think of the toll that success can take on their health. Health expert A.J. Reb Materi said, *"So many people spend their health gaining wealth, and then have to spend their wealth to regain their health."* How much better it is to be health conscious at the start and develop healthy habits that will pay off in the end.

Health goals are things like:

- Diet
- Exercise
- Sleep
- Healthy habits
- Yearly checkups
- Visits to the doctor or a health expert
- Understanding and following alternative methods of healthy living
- Exercise program or gym membership
- Breaking of unhealthy habits like smoking, too much alcohol, the use of recreational drugs, and overeating

Keeping healthy is more than just something good to do. Your life depends on it. Success means nothing if you're hospitalized or dead. Think of getting ready for success as preparing for a triathlon. You have to disciple yourself and work months before the event or you will never make it to the end. Be good to yourself. As Jim Rohn said, *"Take care of your body. It's the only place you have to live."*

7. Fun Goals

"Fun is good!" said Dr. Seuss. You have to have some fun in your life or you will never make it to success. Fun goals are the things you want to do for no other reason than that they are fun. Fun goals help us to relax, take life as it comes and to recharge when needed. If you set aside time to deliberately have fun then you will find you have fun all the time.

Fun goals can be:

- Gardening
- Learning to paint
- Doing crafts
- Taking a trip
- Going away for the day
- A picnic with people you love to be with

Fun goals do not have any set requirements and unlike all the other goals, they do not have to move you anywhere. Fun goals have only one purpose: to have fun.

Unbelievably, many success-minded people have trouble with the idea of just having fun. They seem to think that if they are not working on their goals that they are wasting time. What they fail to see is that fun is never a waste of time. It is the best investment of time in yourself that you can make. You have to have fun or the rest of the journey is nothing but a burden. As Michael Jordan said, *"Just play. Have fun. Enjoy the game."*

Chapter Four

In Closing

Now you have the information you need to set your goals and start moving toward their achievement. I know it can seem a bit overwhelming at first, but as you make this process a habit you will find it quickly becomes a natural part of your life. I have been setting goals for over fifty years now. I was fortunate to discover the process when I was young and it has served me well. I have tried many methods and have had my share of successes and failures, but I always learned. For those who wish to achieve their dream and experience success in life, goal setting cannot be overlooked.

I am reminded of a quote from Henry David Thoreau, *"If one advances confidently in the direction of his dream, and endeavors to live a life which he has imagined, he will meet with a success unexpected in common hours."* My prayer—my desire—for you is that you will meet with an unexpected success. I want you to discover those seeds of greatness that are in you and I want all your dreams to become reality.

There is so much more to be said on the importance of goal setting and the principles of achievement. I am giving you a humble view of a vast topic. Please, I encourage you to become an avid reader. There is a fortune of material in print that will give you more tools than you could ever use. Each of us is unique and what methods work for one may not work as well for another. Thank God we have so much to choose from and so many great teachers from the past and present to help us.

I believe in you! I really do. I know the potential that lies in you and the power that is waiting to be freed in your life. Among those who read this will be the people who change the world. They will be the ones who are not held back by circumstances, other people's restrictions, or lack of ideas. These success-minded people of vision and passion will not be stopped. Winston Churchill said, *"A man with a vision is not held hostage by circumstances."* I believe that person is you.

Thank you for spending this time with me. I have been honored to be able to share with you and I am confident that it has been profitable for you. Allow me to close with a quote from Pastor and author T.D. Jakes. This is what I would like to tell you in person if I could:

"The future is before you like an uninhabited land

waiting for pioneers of destiny to explore it.

Forge ahead!"

More About the Author

John Patrick Hickey has been coaching leaders and individuals and building teams for three decades. He has a personal passion to help Success-Minded People identify their gift, set goals, and achieve their dreams, while becoming the best they can be. John Patrick is a gifted team coach and knows how to help leaders build teams that enrich all their members and that accomplish their objectives. Having been a pastor for several years, John Patrick knows how to work with churches as well as businesses and groups.

John Patrick Hickey is a Certified Life Coach as well as being certified in DISC Assessments and evaluations. He is also an author, instructor, and well-read blogger.

John Patrick and his wife Kate are natives of Michigan. He has two daughters who are both married and have blessed John and Kate with nine grandchildren.